PREVENT

By day: A light but superbly effective moisturizer that's your skin's first line of defense against everyday sun and pollution. Use it alone or under makeup, but never be without it. SPF 15 for everyday, year-round protection. Enriched with vitamins which are natural anti-oxidants to boost skin's defenses.

POND'S®

AGE DEFYING SYSTEM

☀ PREVENT ☀

☾ CORRECT ☾

CORRECT

By night: A richer formulation, but still quickly and easily absorbed. Correct works while you sleep – delivering 3 alpha hydroxys and vitamins to help undo the signs of premature aging, smoothing, firming, encouraging newer skin cells to emerge, creating new radiance. Wake up. It's a new day for your skin.

All Things Sweet

Front cover: Rich Chocolate Layer Cake, page 19; photography by Howard L. Puckett; styling by Ashley J. Wyatt; food styling by Iris Crawley O'Brien

Editor: **Alyson Moreland Haynes**
Art Director: **Amy Heise**
Assistant Art Director: **Craig Hyde**
Managing Editor: **Kay Fuston**
Senior Writer: **Kate Neale Cooper**
Assistant Food Editor: **Regan Miller, R.D.**
Copy Editors: **Maria Parker Hopkins, Carol Boker**
Copy/Production Assistant: **Kate McWhorter**
Food Intern: **Kristi Crowe**
Art Intern: **Chris McDonald**
Copy Intern: **Candace Wilkes**

Photographers: **Ralph Anderson, Jim Bathie, Tina Cornett, Colleen Duffley, Becky Luigart-Stayner, Randy Mayor, Howard L. Puckett**
Photo Stylists: **Cindy Manning Barr, Kay E. Clarke, Melanie J. Clarke, Virginia R. Cravens, Mary Catherine Muir, Fonda Shaia, Ashley J. Wyatt**
Food Stylist: **Iris Crawley O'Brien**

Weight Watchers Magazine Test Kitchens Director: **Kathleen Royal Phillips**
Assistant Director: **Gayle Hays Sadler** Staff: **Julie Christopher, Natalie E. King, L. Victoria Knowles, Rebecca W. Mohr, Jan A. Smith, Kate M. Wheeler, R.D.**

Editor, *Weight Watchers* Magazine: **Kate Greer**
Executive Editor: **Mary Kay Culpepper**
Art Director: **Jamie Ezra Mark**
Articles Editor: **Matthew Solan**
Assistant Editor: **Joe Watts**
Editorial Coordinator: **Christine O'Connell**

Senior Vice President, Publisher: **Jeffrey C. Ward**
General Manager: **Vicki A. Denmark**
Business Manager: **Michael W. Stern**
Marketing Manager: **Betsey Hummel**
Assistant Production Manager: **Robin Boteler**

President and CEO: **Tom Angelillo**
Executive Vice Presidents: **Bruce Akin, Scott Sheppard, Jeanetta Keller**
Vice President, Administration: **Lane Schmitt**
Vice President, Corporate Marketing: **Greg Keyes**
Vice President, Consumer Marketing: **Hallett Johnson III**
Vice President, Circulation: **Pat Vander Meer**
Vice President, Magazine Production: **Larry Rinehart**
Vice President, Finance: **Bruce Larson**

Back cover: Banana Cream Pie, page 30.
Photography: Howard L. Puckett; styling: Ashley J. Wyatt; food styling: Iris Crawley O'Brien.

Weight Watchers Magazine.

WELCOME

Desserts serve many purposes in our lives. Sometimes they're a celebration—a monument to some marital milestone or benchmark birthday; sometimes they're a reward—a prize for a promotion or a treat for accomplishing some lofty (or not-so-lofty) goal; but most importantly they're a way of prolonging a lovely evening with family or friends, an invitation to guests looking for an excuse to linger a little longer, an opportunity to finish a conversation you should have had years ago.

It's our belief that you shouldn't miss out on all those rituals just because you're trying to eat well. That's why we created *All Things Sweet*, a desserts-only cookbook. Moderation, not elimination, should be your goal as far as sweets are concerned. How? Make trade-offs to keep your meals and snacks in balance, and choose desserts lower in fat and calories such as those found in this book.

Back in 1987 when I started working in our company's test kitchen there was no such thing as fat-free sour cream, and fat-free sweetened condensed skim milk didn't exist. We struggled to lighten heavy recipes, using several ingredients to compensate for one heavy product, cooking by trial and error, and failing as often as we succeeded. But that was 12 years ago; today, products and techniques have finally caught up with our desire to indulge in dessert without sacrificing flavor. Today's light recipes, including the more than 130 dessert recipes in this book, are less labor-intensive and, even more importantly, more closely resemble the original recipes we set out to lighten. In fact, we bet you'll have a hard time distinguishing our Chocolate Pound Cake from your grandmother's. But be prepared to share the recipe, just like Grandma did.

Alyson M. Haynes

All Things Sweet

c o n t e n t s

Cakes   6

A Slice of Heaven: Life's too short to save these sweet treats for special occasions.

Pies and Cobblers   22

Comfort in a Crust: Even the most time-honored traditional recipes can be improved upon.

Cookies   38

Stacked in Your Favor: When you have places to go and people to see, you can't beat cookies.

Custards and Puddings   54

Spoon Foods: Put your spoon to good use with these creamy indulgences.

Frozen Desserts   66

Ice Caps: There's no better way to end the day than with one of these cool treats.

Still More Sweets   80

Surprise Endings: Expand your culinary horizons with these unpredictable desserts.

Glossary   94

About Our Recipes   95

Recipe Index   96

A Slice of Heaven

LIFE'S TOO SHORT TO SAVE THESE
SWEET TREATS FOR SPECIAL OCCASIONS.

I n an effort to make special occasions truly special, we sometimes deny

ourselves occasional indulgences. For instance, there's the china that

hasn't left the china cabinet in years and the cake stand that only gets used

when someone's celebrating a birthday or a promotion. There are times when

that approach makes sense—who'd want to hand wash a sterling silver spoon

every time you stir some sugar into your tea? But there are days when "just

A cinch to make, because" should be reason enough to set the table with china or bake a cake.

Orange-Coconut

Angel Food Cake The recipes on these pages, from Chocolate Roulade With Raspberries to New

uses cake and

pudding mixes. York Cheesecake, are reason enough to celebrate.

Caramel-Pineapple
Upside-Down Cake

Orange-Coconut Angel Food Cake

1 (16-ounce) package angel food cake mix
1 cup water
⅓ cup fresh orange juice
2 teaspoons orange extract, divided
1 (3.4-ounce) package French vanilla instant pudding mix
1¾ cups skim milk
1 tablespoon grated orange rind
2 cups flaked sweetened coconut, divided
3¼ cups frozen reduced-calorie whipped topping, thawed and divided

1. Preheat oven to 375°.

2. Prepare angel food cake batter according to package directions, using 1 cup water and ⅓ cup orange juice instead of liquid called for in package directions. Fold 1 teaspoon orange extract into batter. Spoon into an ungreased 10-inch tube pan, spreading evenly. Break air pockets by cutting through batter with a knife. Bake at 375° on lowest oven rack for 30 minutes or until cake springs back when touched lightly in center.

3. Remove cake from oven; invert pan, and let cake cool completely upside-down in pan. Loosen cake from sides of pan using a long narrow metal spatula; remove from pan. Slice cake horizontally into 4 equal layers using a serrated knife; set aside.

4. Prepare instant pudding mix according to package directions, using 1¾ cups skim milk instead of liquid called for on package directions. Stir in remaining 1 teaspoon orange extract and orange rind. Fold in 1 cup coconut and ¾ cup whipped topping. Chill at least 15 minutes.

5. Place bottom cake layer on a serving platter; spread with one-third of pudding mixture. Repeat procedure with remaining cake layers and pudding mixture, ending with top cake layer.

6. Spread remaining 2½ cups whipped topping over top, sides, and inside hole of cake; sprinkle with remaining 1 cup coconut. Store loosely covered in refrigerator. Yield: 16 servings.

POINTS: 4; **Exchanges:** 2½ Starch, ½ Fat
Per serving: CAL 213 (2% from fat); PRO 5.1g; FAT 0.4g (sat 0.1g); CARB 32.3g; FIB 0.1g; CHOL 0mg; IRON 1.4mg; SOD 54mg; CALC 54mg

Caramel-Pineapple Upside-Down Cake

1 (15¼-ounce) can pineapple slices in juice, undrained
½ cup sugar
2½ tablespoons water
¼ cup stick margarine, divided
Cooking spray
9 maraschino cherry halves
1¼ cups all-purpose flour
½ teaspoon baking soda
½ teaspoon baking powder
¼ teaspoon salt
½ cup firmly packed brown sugar
1 large egg
1 large egg white
½ cup low-fat buttermilk
½ teaspoon vanilla extract

1. Drain pineapple, reserving ¼ cup juice. Set aside 5 pineapple slices, reserving remaining slices for another use.

2. Place sugar and water in a heavy saucepan over medium-low heat; cook 6 minutes or until sugar dissolves. Cover, increase heat to medium, and cook 1 minute. Uncover and cook an additional 5 minutes or until golden. Remove from heat; let stand 1 minute. Stir in 1 tablespoon margarine. Gradually stir in reserved ¼ cup pineapple juice (caramelized sugar will harden and stick to spoon). Place over medium heat; cook 3 minutes or until caramelized sugar melts, stirring constantly. Immediately pour into a 9-inch round cake pan coated with cooking spray, tipping quickly until caramelized sugar coats bottom of pan.

3. Place 1 pineapple slice in center of pan; cut remaining slices in half, and arrange in a spoke design around center slice. Place a cherry half in center of each slice; set aside.

4. Preheat oven to 350°.

5. Combine flour and next 3 ingredients; set aside. Beat remaining 3 tablespoons margarine and brown sugar at medium speed of a mixer until creamy. Add egg and egg white, beating well. Add flour mixture to margarine mixture alternately with buttermilk, beginning and ending with

Chocolate Pound Cake travels well to parties and family gatherings.

flour mixture. Stir in vanilla; pour over pineapple.

6. Bake at 350° for 30 minutes or until a wooden pick inserted in center comes out clean. Let cool in pan 5 minutes. Place a plate upside down on top of pan; invert cake onto plate. Serve warm. Yield: 10 servings (serving size: 1 wedge).

POINTS: 5; **Exchanges:** 2 Starch, ½ Fruit, ½ Fat
Per serving: CAL 214 (23% from fat); PRO 3.1g; FAT 5.4g (sat 1.1g); CARB 38.3g; FIB 0.5g; CHOL 22mg; IRON 1.2mg; SOD 221mg; CALC 47mg

Brownie Snack Cake

The spiderweb design on the top of this cake is an easy touch for Halloween.

¾ cup sugar
¼ cup vegetable oil
¼ cup plain fat-free yogurt
1 teaspoon vanilla extract
3 large egg whites
½ cup all-purpose flour
⅓ cup unsweetened cocoa
¼ teaspoon salt
¼ teaspoon baking powder
Cooking spray
1½ cups powdered sugar
2½ tablespoons skim milk
1 teaspoon unsweetened cocoa

1. Preheat oven to 375°.

2. Combine first 5 ingredients in a medium bowl; beat at medium speed of a mixer until well blended. Combine flour, ⅓ cup cocoa, salt, and

baking powder; stir well. Add flour mixture to sugar mixture, beating just until blended.

3. Pour batter into a 9-inch round cake pan coated with cooking spray. Bake at 375° for 25 minutes or until a wooden pick inserted in center comes out clean. Cool in pan 10 minutes; remove from pan, and let cool completely on a wire rack.

4. Combine powdered sugar and milk; beat at low speed of a mixer until smooth. Spread ½ cup powdered sugar glaze over top of cake. Add 1 teaspoon cocoa to remaining powdered sugar glaze, stirring with a whisk until blended. Spoon into a small zip-top plastic bag. Snip off 1 corner of bag, making a small hole. Starting in center of cake, pipe chocolate glaze in 4 concentric circles. Starting at center circle, pull a wooden pick or tip of a knife through circles at regular intervals to edge of cake to form a "web" design. Yield: 12 servings.

POINTS: 4; **Exchanges:** 2 Starch, 1 Fat
Per serving: CAL 186 (24% from fat); PRO 2.5g; FAT 5g (sat 1g); CARB 33.3g; FIB 0.1g; CHOL 0mg; IRON 0.7mg; SOD 69mg; CALC 25mg

Chocolate Pound Cake

Use cooking spray and 1 teaspoon of flour to dust the pan if baking spray isn't available.

¾ cup stick margarine, softened
1½ cups sugar
2 large eggs
2 large egg whites
1½ cups low-fat buttermilk
1 teaspoon baking soda
3½ cups all-purpose flour
¾ cup unsweetened cocoa
1 teaspoon baking powder
¼ teaspoon salt
2 teaspoons vanilla extract
Baking spray with flour
1 teaspoon powdered sugar

1. Preheat oven to 350°.

2. Cream margarine. Gradually add sugar, beating at medium speed of a mixer until well blended. Add eggs and egg whites, 1 at a time, beating well after each addition.

3. Combine buttermilk and baking soda; stir well, and set aside. Combine flour, cocoa, baking powder, and salt; stir well. Add flour mixture to creamed mixture alternately with buttermilk mixture, beginning and ending with flour mixture. Stir in vanilla.

4. Pour batter into a 12-cup Bundt pan coated with baking spray. Bake at 350° for 45 minutes or until a wooden pick inserted in center comes out clean. Let cool in pan 10 minutes on a wire rack; remove from pan. Let cool completely on wire rack. Sift powdered sugar over cake. Yield: 18 servings.

POINTS: 6; **Exchanges:** 2½ Starch, 1½ Fat
Per serving: CAL 259 (32% from fat); PRO 5.4g; FAT 9.2g (sat 2.2g); CARB 38.4g; FIB .6g; CHOL 25mg; IRON 1.8mg; SOD 217mg; CALC 55mg

Lemon Chiffon Cake With Fresh-Fruit Compote

1   cup sifted cake flour
½   cup granulated sugar
1   teaspoon baking powder
¼   teaspoon salt
2   tablespoons vegetable oil
1   tablespoon grated lemon rind
¼   cup fresh lemon juice
1   teaspoon vanilla extract
2   large egg yolks
6   large egg whites (at room temperature)
¼   teaspoon cream of tartar
1   cup sliced fresh strawberries
1   cup fresh blackberries
¼   cup brandy
1   teaspoon granulated sugar
1   tablespoon powdered sugar

1. Preheat oven to 350°.

2. Combine first 4 ingredients in a large bowl; stir well. Add oil, lemon rind, lemon juice, vanilla, and egg yolks; beat at medium speed of a mixer until smooth. Set aside.

3. Beat egg whites and cream of tartar with clean, dry beaters at high speed of mixer until stiff peaks form. Gently stir one-fourth of egg white mixture into batter; gently fold in remaining egg white mixture. Spoon batter into an ungreased 10-inch tube pan, spreading evenly; break air pockets by cutting through batter with a knife. Bake at 350° for 25 minutes or until cake springs back when touched lightly in center. Invert pan; let cool upside-down in pan 40 minutes. Loosen cake from sides of pan using a long narrow metal spatula; remove cake from pan. Place on a cake plate; set aside.

4. Combine berries, brandy, and 1 teaspoon granulated sugar in a medium bowl; stir gently. Let stand at room temperature for 30 minutes. Sift powdered sugar over cake; serve with berry mixture. Yield: 8 servings (serving size: 1 cake slice and ¼ cup berry mixture).

POINTS: 4; **Exchanges:** 1½ Starch, 1 Fat, ½ Fruit
Per serving: CAL 197 (23% from fat); PRO 4.6g; FAT 5g (sat 1g); CARB 29.6g; FIB 1.8g; CHOL 54mg; IRON 1.4mg; SOD 115mg; CALC 53mg

Dark-Chocolate Soufflé Cake

Cooking spray
½   cup granulated sugar
½   cup firmly packed dark brown sugar
¾   cup water
1   tablespoon instant espresso or 2 tablespoons instant coffee granules
⅔   cup Dutch process or unsweetened cocoa
¼   teaspoon salt
2   ounces semisweet chocolate, chopped
2   ounces unsweetened chocolate, chopped
2   tablespoons Kahlúa (coffee-flavored liqueur)
3   large egg yolks
⅓   cup sifted cake flour (such as Swan's Down)
6   large egg whites (at room temperature)
¼   teaspoon cream of tartar
⅓   cup granulated sugar
1   tablespoon powdered sugar
¼   cup fresh raspberries (optional)
Chocolate curls (optional)

1. Preheat oven to 300°.

2. Coat bottom of a 9-inch springform pan with cooking spray; set aside.

3. Combine ½ cup granulated sugar, ½ cup brown sugar, water, and espresso in a large saucepan; stir well, and bring to a boil. Remove from heat; add cocoa and next 3 ingredients, stirring with a whisk until chocolate melts. Stir in Kahlúa and egg yolks. Stir in flour; let cool to room temperature. Set aside.

4. Beat egg whites and cream of tartar with clean, dry beaters at high speed of a mixer until foamy. Add ⅓ cup granulated sugar, 1 tablespoon at a time, beating until stiff peaks form. Gently fold one-fourth of egg white mixture into chocolate mixture; repeat procedure with remaining egg white mixture, one-fourth at a time. Spoon into prepared pan. Bake at 300° for 1 hour or until a wooden pick inserted in center comes out almost clean (some moist crumbs will stick to pick). Let cool completely on wire rack. Remove sides from pan; sift powdered sugar over cake. Garnish with raspberries and chocolate curls, if desired. Yield: 12 servings (serving size: 1 wedge).

Note: A substitution of ¼ cup sifted all-purpose flour may be used in place of ⅓ cup cake flour.

POINTS: 5; **Exchanges:** 2 Starch, 1 Fat
Per serving: CAL 205 (27% from fat); PRO 5g; FAT 6.1g (sat 3.2g); CARB 34.2g; FIB 0.2g; CHOL 55mg; IRON 2mg; SOD 91; CALC 31mg

Cinnamon-Apple Cake

This cake is usually served at Hanukkah. The cream cheese in the batter gives the cake lots of moisture. Because it's so tender, use a serrated knife for cutting.

As Cinnamon-Apple Cake bakes, a sugary crust forms on top.

1¾ cups sugar, divided
½ cup stick margarine, softened
1 teaspoon vanilla extract
6 ounces block-style fat-free cream cheese, softened (about ¾ cup)
2 large eggs
1½ cups all-purpose flour
1½ teaspoons baking powder
¼ teaspoon salt
2 teaspoons ground cinnamon
3 cups peeled chopped Rome apple (about 2 large)
Cooking spray

1. Preheat oven to 350°.

2. Beat 1½ cups sugar, margarine, vanilla, and cream cheese at medium speed of a mixer until well blended (about 4 minutes). Add eggs, 1 at a time, beating well after each addition. Combine flour, baking powder, and salt. Add flour mixture to creamed mixture, beating at low speed until blended.

3. Combine remaining ¼ cup sugar and cinnamon; stir well. Combine 2 tablespoons cinnamon mixture and apple in a bowl; stir apple mixture into batter. Pour batter into an 8-inch springform pan coated with cooking spray, and sprinkle with remaining cinnamon mixture.

4. Bake at 350° for 1 hour and 15 minutes or until cake pulls away from the sides of the pan. Let cool completely on a wire rack; cut with a serrated knife. Yield: 12 servings.

Note: You can also make this cake in a 9-inch square cake pan or a 9-inch springform pan; just reduce the cooking time by 5 minutes.

POINTS: 6; **Exchanges:** 2½ Starch, 1 Fat, ½ Very Lean Meat, ½ Fruit
Per serving: CAL 281 (28% from fat); PRO 4.8g; FAT 8.7g (sat 1.8g); CARB 46.3g; FIB 1.2g; CHOL 39mg; IRON 1.1mg; SOD 234mg; CALC 89mg

Semolina Pudding Cake

A typically simple farm dessert, this cake is a cross between a pudding cake and a soufflé. Look for semolina flour next to the flour and sugar in large supermarkets. And don't worry about testing this cake for doneness. Instead, trust the time and temperature so you don't overcook it. If you insert a toothpick into the cake, the center will always be soft.

1 cup sugar, divided
Cooking spray
4 cups skim milk
1 (3-inch) piece vanilla bean, split
 lengthwise, or 1 tablespoon vanilla
 extract
¾ cup plus 1 tablespoon semolina flour
 (pasta flour)
Dash of salt
3 large eggs, lightly beaten
¼ teaspoon ground nutmeg

1. Place ½ cup sugar in a small heavy saucepan over medium heat, and cook until sugar is golden (about 5 minutes). Immediately pour sugar syrup into a 1½-quart soufflé dish coated with cooking spray, tipping quickly until caramelized sugar coats bottom of dish; set aside.

2. Combine milk and remaining ½ cup sugar in a large heavy saucepan; stir well. Scrape seeds from vanilla bean; add seeds and bean to milk mixture (if using extract in place of vanilla bean, do not add at this point). Cook over medium-high heat to 180° or until tiny bubbles form around edge of pan (do not boil). Remove from heat (add extract at this point if using); cover and let stand 10 minutes. Discard bean.

3. Preheat oven to 375°.

4. Place milk mixture over medium heat. Gradually add flour and salt, stirring constantly with a whisk. Cook 12 minutes or until mixture is thick and bubbly, stirring constantly. Gradually add hot milk mixture to eggs, stirring constantly with a whisk; stir in nutmeg. Spoon mixture into prepared dish.

5. Bake at 375° for 45 minutes or until puffy and almost set (cake will still jiggle slightly in center). Let cool in dish 5 minutes (cake will deflate slightly upon standing). Loosen cake from sides of dish using a narrow metal spatula. Place a plate upside down on top of dish; invert cake onto plate. Serve warm or chilled. Yield: 8 servings.

POINTS: 5; **Exchanges:** 2½ Starch, ½ Sk Milk
Per serving: CAL 238 (10% from fat); PRO 8.8g; FAT 2.6g (sat 1g); CARB 44.5g; FIB 0.6g; CHOL 85mg; IRON 0.4mg; SOD 92mg; CALC 160mg

Oat Cake With Coconut-Nut Topping

Cooking spray
2 teaspoons all-purpose flour
⅓ cup 1% low-fat milk
¼ cup regular oats
¾ cup all-purpose flour
1 teaspoon baking powder
½ teaspoon ground cinnamon
¼ teaspoon salt
½ cup granulated sugar
2 tablespoons stick margarine, softened
⅓ cup applesauce
1 teaspoon vanilla extract
1 large egg
⅓ cup firmly packed dark brown sugar
¼ cup evaporated skim milk
1 tablespoon stick margarine
¼ cup regular oats
¼ cup shredded sweetened coconut
3 tablespoons finely chopped walnuts

1. Preheat oven to 350°.

2. Coat an 8-inch round cake pan with cooking spray; dust with 2 teaspoons flour, and set aside.

3. Bring 1% low-fat milk to a simmer in a small saucepan; stir in ¼ cup oats. Bring mixture to a boil, and remove from heat. Spoon mixture into a small bowl; let cool.

4. Combine ¾ cup flour, baking powder, cinnamon, and salt in a bowl; set aside. Combine ½ cup granulated sugar and 2 tablespoons softened

Dense and moist, Oat Cake With Coconut-Nut Topping is true comfort food.

margarine in a large bowl; beat at medium speed of a mixer until blended. Add applesauce, vanilla, and egg; beat until blended. Add flour mixture and oatmeal mixture; beat until well blended. Pour into prepared pan. Bake at 350° for 25 minutes or until a wooden pick inserted in center comes out clean. Remove from oven; place on a wire rack.

5. Combine brown sugar, evaporated milk, and 1 tablespoon margarine in a small saucepan; bring to a boil over medium heat, and cook 30 seconds. Stir in ¼ cup oats, coconut, and walnuts; cook 30 seconds. Spread over cake; broil 2 minutes or until lightly browned. Let cool. Yield: 8 servings.

POINTS: 5; Exchanges: 2½ Starch, 1 Fat
Per serving: CAL 245 (26% from fat); PRO 4.7g; FAT 8.2g (sat 2.1g); CARB 38.9g; FIB 1.4g; CHOL 28mg; IRON 1.4mg; SOD 158mg; CALC 91mg

Triple-Chocolate Cheesecake
This cheesecake tastes like a frozen fudge pop.

¼ cup sugar
1 tablespoon stick margarine
1 tablespoon egg white
1⅓ cups chocolate graham cracker crumbs (about 16 crackers)
Cooking spray
3 tablespoons dark rum
3 (1-ounce) squares semisweet chocolate
¼ cup chocolate-flavored syrup
1 (8-ounce) block fat-free cream cheese, softened
1 (8-ounce) package Neufchâtel cheese or light cream cheese, softened
1 cup sugar
2 tablespoons unsweetened cocoa
1 teaspoon vanilla extract
¼ teaspoon salt
2 large eggs
½ cup low-fat sour cream
1 tablespoon sugar
2 teaspoons unsweetened cocoa
Chocolate curls (optional)

1. Preheat oven to 350°.

2. Place first 3 ingredients in a bowl; beat at medium speed of a mixer until blended. Stir in crumbs. Press mixture into bottom and 1 inch up sides of an 8-inch springform pan coated with cooking spray. Bake at 350° for 10 minutes; let cool on a wire rack. Reduce oven temperature to 300°.

3. Combine rum and chocolate squares in the top of a double boiler. Cook over simmering water 2 minutes or until chocolate melts, stirring frequently. Remove from heat; add chocolate syrup, stirring until smooth.

4. Place cheeses in a large bowl; beat at medium speed of a mixer until smooth. Add 1 cup sugar, 2 tablespoons cocoa, vanilla, and salt; beat until smooth. Add rum mixture; beat at low speed until well blended. Add eggs, 1 at a time, beating just until blended after each addition (do not overmix or cake will crack).

5. Pour cheese mixture into prepared pan; bake at 300° for 40 minutes or until almost set (cake will still jiggle in center but will firm up as it cools). Combine sour cream, 1 tablespoon sugar, and 2 teaspoons cocoa; stir well. Turn oven off; remove cheesecake from oven. Spread sour cream mixture over cheesecake; return cheesecake to oven. Let stand for 45 minutes in oven with door closed.

6. Remove cheesecake from oven; run a knife around edge of cake to loosen cake from pan. Let cool to room temperature. Cover and chill at least 8 hours. Garnish with chocolate curls, if desired. Yield: 12 servings.

POINTS: 6; **Exchanges**: 2½ Starch, 2 Fat
Per serving: CAL 260 (35% from fat); PRO 7.5g; FAT 10.1g (sat 5.5g); CARB 35.9g; FIB 0.1g; CHOL 57mg; IRON 0.7mg; SOD 205mg; CALC 85mg

Chocolate Roulade With Raspberries

Cooking spray
2   tablespoons dry breadcrumbs
4   large egg yolks
¾   cup sugar, divided
6   large egg whites (at room temperature)
⅛   teaspoon salt
1   teaspoon vanilla extract
½   cup Dutch process cocoa
2   tablespoons powdered sugar
2   cups frozen reduced-calorie whipped topping, thawed
10 teaspoons chocolate-flavored syrup
2½ cups fresh raspberries

1. Preheat oven to 375°.

2. Coat a 15- x 10-inch jelly-roll pan with cooking spray; line bottom with wax paper. Coat wax paper with cooking spray. Dust with breadcrumbs; set aside.

3. Beat egg yolks in a bowl at high speed of a mixer for 4 minutes. Gradually add ¼ cup sugar, beating until thick and pale (about 2 minutes); set aside. Beat egg whites with clean, dry beaters at high speed of a mixer until foamy; add salt. Gradually add remaining ½ cup sugar, 1 tablespoon at a time, beating until stiff peaks form. Beat in vanilla. Sprinkle cocoa over egg white mixture, and gently fold until well blended. Stir one-fourth of egg white mixture into egg yolk mixture; gently fold in remaining egg white mixture.

4. Spoon batter into prepared pan, spreading evenly to sides of pan. Bake at 375° for 15 minutes or until cake springs back when touched lightly in center. Loosen cake from sides of pan; turn out onto a dishtowel dusted with 2 tablespoons powdered sugar. Carefully peel off wax paper; let cake cool 1 minute. Starting at short end, roll up cake and towel together. Place, seam side down, on a wire rack; let cool completely (about 1 hour).

5. Unroll cake carefully; remove towel. Spread whipped topping over cake, leaving a ½-inch margin around outside edges. Reroll cake; place, seam side down, on a platter. Cover; chill 1 hour. Cut cake into 10 (1-inch) slices. Drizzle 1 teaspoon syrup on each of 10 plates; top with 1 cake slice and ¼ cup raspberries. Yield: 10 servings.

POINTS: 4; **Exchanges**: 1 Starch, 1 Fruit, 1 Fat
Per serving: CAL 181 (24% from fat); PRO 5.4g; FAT 4.8g (sat 2.2g); CARB 29.5g; FIB 1.9g; CHOL 87mg; IRON 1.3mg; SOD 91mg; CALC 36mg

New York Cheesecake

⅔   cup all-purpose flour
2   tablespoons sugar
2   tablespoons chilled stick margarine, cut into small pieces
1   tablespoon ice water
Cooking spray
3   (8-ounce) blocks fat-free cream cheese, softened
2   (8-ounce) packages Neufchâtel cheese or light cream cheese, softened
1¾ cups sugar
3   tablespoons all-purpose flour
1   tablespoon vanilla extract

1 Let egg whites stand at room temperature 20 minutes. Add cream of tartar (if called for); beat with clean, dry beaters at high speed of a mixer until foamy.

2 Add sugar to foamy egg whites as directed.

3 Beat egg white mixture until soft peaks form. The egg whites will gently fold over when beaters are pulled away.

4 With continued beating, the egg whites will form stiff peaks, which will stand up when the beaters are pulled away.

PUMPKIN PURÉE

A three-pound fresh pumpkin yields 3 cups of mashed cooked pumpkin. Fresh cooked pumpkin purée will keep in a sealed container in the refrigerator for about five days or in the freezer for up to six months.

1 Place whole pumpkin on a foil-lined baking sheet. Bake at 350° for 1 hour and 30 minutes or until tender, turning baking sheet occasionally. Remove from oven; let cool.

2 Allow the pumpkin to cool thoroughly, and then remove the seeds and stringy pulp with a large spoon.

3 Remove the peel. Process the flesh in a food processor or by hand (using a potato masher) until smooth.

1½ teaspoons grated orange rind
1 teaspoon grated lemon rind
¼ teaspoon salt
5 large eggs
Lemon zest (optional)
Orange slices (optional)
Lemon slices (optional)

1. Preheat oven to 400°.

2. Place ⅔ cup flour and 2 tablespoons sugar in a food processor; pulse 2 times or until blended. Add chilled margarine; pulse 6 times or until mixture resembles coarse meal. With processor on, slowly pour ice water through food chute, processing just until blended (do not allow dough to form a ball). Firmly press mixture into bottom of a 9-inch springform pan coated with cooking spray. Bake at 400° for 10 minutes; let cool on a wire rack. Increase oven temperature to 525° or to highest oven setting.

3. Place cheeses in a large bowl; beat at high speed of a mixer until smooth. Add 1¾ cups sugar and next 5 ingredients; beat well. Add eggs, 1 at a time, beating just until blended after each addition (do not overmix or cake will crack). Pour cheese mixture into prepared pan; bake at 525° for 7 minutes. Reduce oven temperature to 200°, and bake 45 minutes or until almost set (cake will still jiggle in center but will firm up as it cools).

4. Remove cheesecake from oven; run a knife around edge of cake to loosen cake from pan. Let cool to room temperature. Cover and chill at least 8 hours. Garnish with lemon zest, orange slices, and lemon slices, if desired. Yield: 16 servings.

POINTS: 6; **Exchanges:** 1½ Starch, ½ Low-fat Milk, ½ Hi-fat Meat, ½ Fat
Per serving: CAL 261 (32% from fat); PRO 11.7g; FAT 9.2g (sat 4.8g); CARB 31.4g; FIB 0.2g; CHOL 97mg; IRON 0.6mg; SOD 449mg; CALC 147mg

Irish Fruitcake

Wrap this dense cake in whiskey-soaked cheesecloth for at least 1 week for optimum flavor.

3 cups all-purpose flour
1 teaspoon baking powder
½ teaspoon ground cinnamon

¼ teaspoon ground nutmeg
¼ teaspoon salt
½ cup brownulated granulated sugar
6 tablespoons stick margarine, softened
½ cup Irish whiskey, divided
1 teaspoon almond extract
1 teaspoon vanilla extract
½ teaspoon grated lemon rind
4 large eggs
1 cup skim milk
1½ cups diced Golden Delicious apple
½ cup raisins
½ cup dried currants
⅓ cup quartered red candied cherries
¼ cup candied mixed fruit
Cooking spray
½ cup sifted powdered sugar
2 teaspoons skim milk
8 whole blanched almonds
4 candied red cherries, halved

1. Preheat oven 300°.

2. Combine first 5 ingredients; stir well, and set aside. Cream brownulated sugar and margarine at medium speed of a mixer until light and fluffy (about 5 minutes). Add ¼ cup whiskey and next 4 ingredients; beat at medium speed for 4 minutes or until well blended. Add flour mixture to creamed mixture alternately with milk, beginning and ending with flour mixture. Stir in apple and next 4 ingredients.

3. Spoon batter into a 12-cup Bundt pan coated with cooking spray; bake at 300° for 1 hour and 25 minutes or until a wooden pick inserted in center comes out clean. Cool in pan 10 minutes. Remove from pan; cool completely on a wire rack.

4. Moisten several layers of cheesecloth in remaining ¼ cup whiskey; wrap cake in cheesecloth. Cover completely with plastic wrap and then with foil. Store in a cool, dry place at least 1 week. Unwrap cake. Combine powdered sugar and milk; stir well. Drizzle sugar glaze over cake. Arrange almonds and candied cherries on top of cake. Yield: 20 servings (serving size: 1 slice).

POINTS: 4; **Exchanges:** 2 Starch, ½ Fat
Per serving: CAL 188 (24% from fat); PRO 3.9g; FAT 5.2g (sat 1.1g); CARB 31.5g; FIB 1g; CHOL 43mg; IRON 1.3mg; SOD 113mg; CALC 48mg

Spiced Pumpkin Cake

1⅔ cups all-purpose flour
⅓ cup raisins
¼ cup chopped walnuts
1 teaspoon baking soda
½ teaspoon baking powder
1 cup fresh pumpkin purée or unsweetened canned pumpkin
½ cup firmly packed dark brown sugar
⅓ cup apple juice
¼ cup sugar
¼ cup vegetable oil
1½ teaspoons ground cinnamon
1 teaspoon ground ginger
¼ teaspoon ground nutmeg
1 large egg
1 teaspoon vanilla extract
Cooking spray
1 teaspoon powdered sugar
Lemon rind strips (optional)

1. Preheat oven to 350°.

2. Combine flour, raisins, walnuts, baking soda, and baking powder in a medium bowl; stir well. Combine pumpkin and next 8 ingredients in a large bowl; beat at medium speed of a mixer until well blended. Gradually add flour mixture, beating at low speed. Beat at high speed 2 minutes. Stir in vanilla.

3. Pour batter into a 6-cup Bundt pan coated with cooking spray. Bake at 350° for 50 minutes or until a wooden pick inserted in center comes out clean. Let cake cool in pan 10 minutes on a wire rack. Remove cake from pan; let cool completely on a wire rack. Sift powdered sugar over cake; garnish with lemon rind strips, if desired. Yield: 16 servings.

Note: To prepare this cake ahead of time, wrap the cooled cake in heavy-duty plastic wrap, and then store in the freezer for up to 3 weeks. Let cake stand at room temperature until thawed. Sift 1 teaspoon powdered sugar over cake just before serving, and garnish with lemon rind strips, if desired.

POINTS: 3; **Exchanges:** 1½ Starch, 1 Fat
Per serving: CAL 150 (31% from fat); PRO 2.5g; FAT 5.1g (sat 0.9g); CARB 24.3g; FIB 1.3g; CHOL 14mg; IRON 1.2mg; SOD 87mg; CALC 26mg

Mississippi Mud Cake

Prepare Chocolate Glaze while cake bakes, so it can be immediately drizzled over warm cake.

⅓ cup margarine, softened
1 cup sugar
3 large eggs
1 cup all-purpose flour
⅓ cup unsweetened cocoa
½ teaspoon baking powder
¼ teaspoon salt
½ cup chopped pecans
1 teaspoon vanilla extract
Cooking spray
3¼ cups miniature marshmallows
Chocolate Glaze

1. Preheat oven to 325°.

2. Cream margarine. Gradually add sugar, beating at medium speed of a mixer until well blended. Add eggs, 1 at a time, beating well after each addition.

3. Combine flour and next 3 ingredients; stir well. Add to creamed mixture, beating at low speed until blended. Stir in pecans and vanilla. Pour into a 13- x 9-inch baking dish coated with cooking spray. Bake at 325° for 16 minutes or just

Enjoy Spiced Pumpkin Cake year-round with canned pumpkin.

When an ordinary dessert won't do, try Polenta Cake With Roasted Nectarines.

until set (not until toothpick tests clean or cake will be overbaked).

4. Remove cake from oven, and top with miniature marshmallows. Bake at 325° for 2 minutes or until marshmallows are soft. Remove from oven; drizzle with Chocolate Glaze, and let cool. Yield: 16 servings.

POINTS: 6; **Exchanges:** 3 Starch, 1 Fat
Per serving: CAL 271 (16% from fat); PRO 3.8g; FAT 9.4g (sat 1.9g); CARB 44g; FIB 0.5g; CHOL 42mg; IRON 1.3mg; SOD 118mg; CALC 29mg

Chocolate Glaze:

2   cups sifted powdered sugar
6   tablespoons unsweetened cocoa
¼   cup skim milk
2   tablespoons margarine
1   teaspoon vanilla extract

1. Combine sugar and cocoa in a bowl; stir well. Combine milk and margarine in a 1-cup glass measure. Microwave at HIGH 1 minute or until margarine melts. Add milk mixture and vanilla to sugar mixture; beat at low speed of a mixer until blended. Yield: 1 cup.

Polenta Cake With Roasted Nectarines

⅓   cup stick margarine, softened
⅔   cup firmly packed dark brown sugar, divided
2   large eggs
¼   cup skim milk
½   teaspoon grated lemon rind
1⅔ cups all-purpose flour
¼   cup yellow cornmeal (not self-rising or cornmeal mix)
1   teaspoon baking powder
¼   teaspoon baking soda
¼   teaspoon salt
1¼ cups peeled, finely chopped Granny Smith apple
Cooking spray
¼   cup water
1   teaspoon ground cinnamon
8   medium firm nectarines (about 1½ pounds), halved
1   tablespoon turbinado sugar or granulated sugar
Cinnamon sticks (optional)

1. Preheat oven to 350°.

2. Beat margarine and ⅓ cup brown sugar at medium speed of a mixer until well blended. Add eggs, 1 at a time, beating well after each addition. Add milk and lemon rind; beat well. Combine flour and next 4 ingredients; add to creamed mixture, and beat well. Stir in chopped apple.

3. Spoon batter into a 9-inch round cake pan coated with cooking spray. Bake at 350° for 28 minutes or until a wooden pick inserted in center comes out clean. Let cool in pan 5 minutes; remove from pan. Let cool completely on a wire rack.

4. Preheat oven to 475°.

5. Combine remaining ⅓ cup brown sugar, water, and cinnamon in a 2-cup glass measure; stir well. Microwave at HIGH 30 seconds or until sugar dissolves. Combine nectarines and brown sugar mixture; toss well. Arrange nectarines, cut sides down, in a 13- x 9-inch baking dish. Bake at 475° for 15 minutes or until tender. Turn nectarines over; sprinkle with turbinado sugar. Bake an additional 5 minutes. Serve with cake. Garnish with cinnamon sticks, if desired. Yield: 8 servings (serving size: 1 cake wedge and 2 nectarine halves).

Note: Substitute 6 small, firm Bosc pears, cored and quartered, for nectarines, if desired.

POINTS: 6; Exchanges: 2½ Starch, 1 Fruit, 1 Fat
Per serving: CAL 303 (29% from fat); PRO 5.5g; FAT 9.8g (sat 2g); CARB 49.8g; FIB 3.4g; CHOL 55mg; IRON 2.3mg; SOD 224mg; CALC 67mg

Rich Chocolate Layer Cake

This low-fat chocolate cake will please even the most finicky chocolate lover.

Cooking spray
2   cups sugar
10 tablespoons light butter (such as Land O' Lakes), softened
¾   cup egg substitute
2   cups all-purpose flour
½   cup unsweetened cocoa
¾   teaspoon baking soda
¼   teaspoon salt
¾   cup low-fat sour cream
¾   cup boiling water
1   teaspoon vanilla extract
Chocolate Frosting
18 fresh raspberries
1   ounce white chocolate curls

1. Preheat oven to 350°.

2. Coat bottoms of 2 (8-inch) round cake pans with cooking spray (do not coat sides of pan); line bottoms of pans with wax paper. Coat wax paper with cooking spray; set aside.

3. Beat sugar and butter at medium speed of a mixer until well blended. Gradually add egg substitute; beat well. Combine flour, cocoa, baking soda, and salt in a bowl. Add flour mixture to sugar mixture alternately with sour cream, beginning and ending with flour mixture. Gently stir in boiling water and vanilla.

4. Pour batter into prepared pans. Bake at 350° for 35 minutes or until cake springs back when touched lightly in center. Loosen cake from sides of pans using a narrow metal spatula; invert cake layers onto wire racks. Peel off wax paper; let cool.

5. Place 1 cake layer on a plate; spread with ½ cup Chocolate Frosting. Top with other cake layer; spread remaining frosting over top and sides of cake. Top with raspberries and white chocolate curls. Yield: 18 servings.

POINTS: 7; Exchanges: 4 Starch, 1 Fat
Per serving: CAL 331 (23% from fat); PRO 4g; FAT 8.6g (sat 2g); CARB 59.1g; FIB 0.5g; CHOL 8mg; IRON 1mg; SOD 191mg; CALC 48mg

Chocolate Frosting:

Don't prepare this frosting ahead of time because it's easier to spread when freshly made.

4   ounces tub-style light cream cheese (about ½ cup), softened
3   tablespoons skim milk
3   (1-ounce) squares semisweet chocolate, melted
3   cups sifted powdered sugar
¼   cup unsweetened cocoa
1   teaspoon vanilla extract

1. Beat cream cheese and milk at high speed of a mixer until creamy. Add melted chocolate; beat until well blended.

2. Combine sugar and cocoa; gradually add sugar mixture to cheese mixture, beating at low speed until well blended. Add vanilla; beat well for 1 minute until creamy. Yield: 1¾ cups.

Meaning "beginning of the year," Rosh Hashanah is the Jewish New Year. It is celebrated during the first two days of Tishri, the first month of the Jewish calendar, which corresponds to September or October on our solar calendar. (Because the traditional Jewish calendar is based on the lunar cycle, the various holidays don't always occur on the same date of the 12-month calendar. Desserts tend to be on the sweet side, because the wish is for a sweet year ahead. Honey Cake is a traditional Rosh Hashanah dessert.

Honey Cake

This cake, traditionally served the first night of Rosh Hashanah, expresses hope that the year to come will be sweet. You can make it two to three days ahead of time and store it in a zip-top plastic bag; the flavor actually improves over time.

Cooking spray
1 tablespoon dry breadcrumbs
¼ cup hot water
2 teaspoons instant espresso or 4 teaspoons instant coffee granules
½ cup sugar
2 large eggs
½ cup honey
3 tablespoons stick margarine, melted
1¾ cups all-purpose flour
1 teaspoon baking powder
1 teaspoon ground cinnamon
¼ teaspoon salt
½ cup chopped walnuts
½ cup golden raisins

1. Preheat oven to 325°.

2. Coat an 8- x 4-inch loaf pan with cooking spray, and dust with breadcrumbs; set aside.

3. Combine hot water and instant espresso; stir well, and set aside.

4. Combine sugar and eggs in a medium bowl; stir well with a whisk. Add honey and margarine; stir well. Combine flour, baking powder, cinnamon, and salt. Add half of flour mixture to sugar mixture; stir well. Add coffee mixture; stir well. Add remaining flour mixture, stirring just until moist. Stir in walnuts and raisins.

5. Spoon batter into prepared pan; bake at 325° for 1 hour and 20 minutes or until a wooden pick inserted in center comes out clean. Let cool in pan 10 minutes on a wire rack; remove from pan. Let cool completely on wire rack. Yield: 12 servings.

POINTS: 5; **Exchanges:** 2½ Starch, 1 Fat
Per serving: CAL 236 (26% from fat); PRO 4.7g; FAT 7g (sat 1.1g); CARB 40.9g; FIB 1.3g; CHOL 37mg; IRON 1.5mg; SOD100mg; CALC 42mg

Blueberry-Buttermilk Cake

3½ cups all-purpose flour
1½ cups firmly packed brown sugar
1 teaspoon ground cinnamon
¼ teaspoon ground nutmeg
¼ teaspoon salt
½ cup plus 2 tablespoons chilled stick margarine, cut into small pieces and divided
1½ teaspoons baking powder
½ teaspoon baking soda
1½ cups low-fat buttermilk
½ cup egg substitute
½ cup apple butter
1 teaspoon vanilla extract
½ teaspoon grated lemon rind
Cooking spray
2 cups fresh blueberries

1. Preheat oven to 350°.

2. Combine first 5 ingredients in a large bowl; cut in ½ cup margarine with a pastry blender or 2 knives until mixture resembles coarse meal. Place 1 cup flour mixture in a small bowl, and cut in 2 tablespoons margarine to form a streusel. Set aside.

3. Add baking powder and baking soda to remaining flour mixture in large bowl; stir well. Combine buttermilk, egg substitute, apple butter, vanilla, and lemon rind. Pour buttermilk mixture over flour mixture; beat at low speed of a mixer until well blended.

4. Pour batter into a 13- x 9-inch baking pan coated with cooking spray. Top batter with fresh blueberries, and sprinkle with streusel. Bake at 350° for 50 minutes or until a wooden pick inserted in center comes out clean. Let cake cool in pan on a wire rack. Yield: 16 servings (serving size: 1 piece).

POINTS: 6; **Exchanges:** 2½ Starch, 1 Fat, ½ Fruit,
Per serving: CAL 259 (27% from fat); PRO 4.7g; FAT 7.9g (sat 1.7g); CARB 42.9g; FIB 1.6g; CHOL 0mg; IRON 1.8mg; SOD 189mg; CALC 78mg

Fruited Carrot Cake

This recipe uses 1½ tubs of frosting. Use the leftover frosting to ice brownies or a single layer cake.

1 cup water
2 tablespoons plus 2 teaspoons fat replacement for baking (such as Smucker's)
2 teaspoons grated orange rind

1 (8-ounce) carton egg substitute
1 (18.25-ounce) package spice cake mix
   (such as Duncan Hines Moist Deluxe)
2 cups shredded carrot
½ cup raisins
1 (8-ounce) can unsweetened crushed
   pineapple, drained
Baking spray with flour
2¼ cups chilled cream cheese-flavored frosting
   (such as Duncan Hines Creamy
   Homestyle)
¼ cup chopped pecans

1. Preheat oven to 350°.
2. Combine first 4 ingredients; stir well. Combine cake mix and water mixture in a large bowl; beat at low speed of a mixer until moist (about 30 seconds). Beat at medium speed for 2 minutes. Stir in carrot, raisins, and pineapple. Divide batter evenly among 3 (8-inch) pans coated with baking spray.
3. Bake at 350° for 18 minutes or until a wooden pick inserted in center comes out clean (do not overcook). Let cool in pans on a wire rack 15 minutes. Invert cakes onto wire rack; cool completely.
4. Place 1 cake layer on a serving platter; spread with about ⅓ cup frosting. Top with second cake layer; spread with about ⅓ cup frosting. Top with remaining cake layer; spread with about ½ cup frosting. Spread remaining 1 cup frosting around sides of cake; top with pecans. Cover and chill. Yield: 18 servings.

POINTS: 7; **Exchanges:** 3 Starch, 1 Fat, ½ Fruit
Per serving: CAL 306 (28% from fat); PRO 3g; FAT 9.4g (sat 1.6g); CARB 51.3g; FIB 0.8g; CHOL 0mg; IRON 1mg; SOD 266mg; CALC 75mg

Raspberry-Almond Coffee Cake

With yogurt replacing the traditional sour cream, you'd never guess that this tender confection is light. Not too gooey and not too sweet, this is what a classic coffee cake should be.

1 cup fresh raspberries
3 tablespoons brown sugar
1 cup all-purpose flour
⅓ cup sugar
½ teaspoon baking powder
¼ teaspoon baking soda
⅛ teaspoon salt
½ cup plain low-fat yogurt
2 tablespoons stick margarine, melted
1 teaspoon vanilla extract
1 large egg
Cooking spray
1 tablespoon sliced almonds
¼ cup sifted powdered sugar
1 teaspoon skim milk
¼ teaspoon vanilla extract

1. Preheat oven to 350°.
2. Combine raspberries and brown sugar in a bowl; toss gently, and set aside.
3. Combine flour and next 4 ingredients in a large bowl. Combine yogurt, margarine, 1 teaspoon vanilla, and egg in a small bowl; stir well. Add to flour mixture, stirring just until moist. Spoon two-thirds of batter into an 8-inch round cake pan coated with cooking spray, and spread evenly. Top with raspberry mixture. Spoon remaining batter over raspberry mixture, and top with almonds.
4. Bake at 350° for 40 minutes or until a wooden pick inserted in center comes out clean. Let cool 10 minutes on a wire rack. Combine powdered sugar, milk, and ¼ teaspoon vanilla; stir well. Drizzle over cake. Serve warm or at room temperature. Yield: 8 servings (serving size: 1 wedge).

POINTS: 4; **Exchanges:** 2 Starch, ½ Fat
Per serving: CAL 176 (23% from fat); PRO 3.5g; FAT 4.5g (sat 1g); CARB 30.4g; FIB 1.7g; CHOL 28mg; IRON 1.1mg; SOD131mg; CALC 59mg

Raspberry-Almond Coffee Cake bursts with the sweet, tangy bite of fresh raspberries.

Comfort
In a Crust

EVEN THE MOST TIME-HONORED TRADITIONAL
RECIPES CAN BE IMPROVED UPON.

There's nothing wrong with Mom's pie—it's just that Streusel Apple Pie is so good . . . and so light.

*W*hile pie has been elevated to the status of American icon, its humble cousins, the cobbler and the crumble, and the even lesser-known slumps, grunts, and pings are not quite as exalted. And that's a shame. Because these not-so-distant relatives also pair sweet fillings such as chocolate and fruit, with flaky pastry, tender dough, or crunchy crumbs—the same combination that makes pies so appealing. After all, Blackberry Cobbler without the biscuit crust is just fruit, and Tropical Sundae Pie without the ginger-snap crust is just ice cream. It's the sugary crumble and the buttery crust that prove that sometimes the whole truly is greater than the sum of its parts.

Keep Tropical Sundae Pie in the freezer, ready to serve when you need a cool treat.

Streusel Apple Pie

For pie à la mode, top each warm slice with a small scoop of vanilla low-fat ice cream or frozen yogurt, and sprinkle with ground nutmeg.

Food Processor Pastry
1   (4-inch) piece vanilla bean, split lengthwise
¼   cup firmly packed brown sugar
1½ tablespoons all-purpose flour
½   teaspoon ground cinnamon
2½ pounds Rome or other cooking apple, peeled, cored, and thinly sliced
½   cup firmly packed brown sugar
¼   cup all-purpose flour
¼   cup regular oats
¼   teaspoon ground cinnamon
3   tablespoons chilled stick margarine, cut into small pieces

1. Prepare Food Processor Pastry; set aside (do not bake).

2. Preheat oven to 350°.

3. Scrape seeds from vanilla bean into a large bowl; discard bean. Add ¼ cup brown sugar, 1½ tablespoons flour, and ½ teaspoon cinnamon to vanilla seeds; stir well. Add apple slices; toss well to coat. Spoon mixture into prepared pastry crust. Cover with foil, and bake at 350° for 45 minutes or until apple mixture is crisp-tender.

4. Combine ½ cup brown sugar and next 3 ingredients; cut in margarine with a pastry blender or 2 knives until mixture is crumbly. Uncover pie, and sprinkle with oats mixture. Bake, uncovered, at 350° for an additional 25 minutes. Yield: 8 servings.

Note: Substitute 1 teaspoon vanilla extract for vanilla bean, if desired.

POINTS: 6; **Exchanges:** 2½ Starch, 1 Fruit, 1 Fat
Per serving: CAL 308 (27% from fat); PRO 2.8g; FAT 9.1g (sat 1.8g); CARB 56.2g; FIB 3g; CHOL 0mg; IRON 1.6mg; SOD 132mg; CALC 27mg

Food Processor Pastry:

1   cup all-purpose flour
1   teaspoon sugar
¼   teaspoon salt
3   tablespoons vegetable shortening
3½   tablespoons ice water
Cooking spray

1. Place first 3 ingredients in a food processor; pulse 3 times or until blended. Add shortening; pulse 6 times or until mixture resembles coarse meal. With processor on, slowly pour ice water through food chute, processing just until combined (do not form a ball).

2. Press mixture gently into a 4-inch circle on heavy-duty plastic wrap; cover with additional plastic wrap. Roll dough, still covered, into an 11-inch circle; chill 10 minutes or until plastic wrap can be easily removed. Remove plastic wrap; fit dough into a 9-inch pie plate coated with cooking spray. Fold edges under, and flute. Yield: 1 (9-inch) pastry crust.

Tropical Sundae Pie

1½   cups diced fresh pineapple
¼   cup sugar
3   tablespoons white rum
24   gingersnaps
1   tablespoon stick margarine, melted
1   large egg white
Cooking spray
4   cups vanilla low-fat frozen yogurt, softened
2   tablespoons sliced almonds, toasted
2   tablespoons flaked sweetened coconut, toasted
Fresh pineapple chunks (optional)

1. Combine diced pineapple and sugar in a small saucepan; bring to a boil. Reduce heat to medium, and cook 10 minutes or until reduced to 1 cup. Remove from heat, and stir in rum. Let cool completely; set aside.

2. Preheat oven to 350°.

3. Place an extra-large bowl in freezer.

4. Place gingersnaps in a food processor; process until crumbly. Add margarine and egg white; pulse

5 times or just until moist. Press crumb mixture evenly into a 9-inch pie plate coated with cooking spray. Bake at 350° for 7 minutes; let cool on a wire rack 15 minutes. Freeze piecrust 30 minutes.

5. Spoon yogurt into chilled extra-large bowl; fold in pineapple mixture. Freeze 30 minutes or just until set but not solid. Spoon yogurt mixture into prepared crust. Sprinkle mixture with almonds and coconut; freeze until set. Cover with plastic wrap, and freeze 6 hours or until firm.

6. Place pie in refrigerator 30 minutes before serving to soften. Garnish with pineapple chunks, if desired. Yield: 8 servings.

POINTS: 6; **Exchanges:** 3 Starch, 1 Fat
Per serving: CAL 281 (29% from fat); PRO 5.1g; FAT 8.7g (sat 3.1g); CARB 43.2g; FIB 0.7g; CHOL 18mg; IRON 1.4mg; SOD 91mg; CALC 139mg

Raspberry Chiffon Pie

2   tablespoons reduced-calorie stick margarine
1   cup crushed vanilla wafers
2   cups fresh raspberries
⅓   cup sugar
⅓   cup skim milk
½   teaspoon vanilla extract
¼   teaspoon salt
2   large egg yolks
1   envelope unflavored gelatin
2   large egg whites (at room temperature)
¼   teaspoon cream of tartar
2   tablespoons sugar
Fresh raspberries (optional)
Mint sprigs (optional)

1. Place margarine in a 9-inch pie plate. Microwave at HIGH 30 seconds or until margarine melts. Add crushed wafers; stir well. Press mixture evenly over bottom and up sides of pie plate. Microwave at HIGH 1 to 2 minutes or until firm, rotating pie plate a half-turn every 30 seconds.

2. Place raspberries in a blender; process until smooth. Strain purée, discarding seeds. Combine purée, ⅓ cup sugar, and next 5 ingredients in a 1½-quart baking dish. Microwave at MEDIUM (50% power) 4 to 6 minutes or until mixture boils, stirring every 2 minutes. Let stand 30 to

2 large egg whites
3 tablespoons skim milk, divided
2 tablespoons unsweetened cocoa
Chocolate syrup (optional)
Fresh raspberries (optional)

1. Preheat oven to 425°.

2. Combine first 4 ingredients in a bowl. Firmly press mixture into bottom and 1 inch up sides of a 9-inch springform pan coated with cooking spray. Set aside.

3. Combine ½ cup sugar, flour, vanilla, and cheeses; beat at medium speed of a mixer until well blended. Add egg whites and 2 tablespoons milk; beat well. Combine ½ cup batter, remaining 1 tablespoon milk, remaining 2 tablespoons sugar, and cocoa in a small bowl; stir well. Spoon remaining batter alternately with cocoa mixture into prepared crust. Swirl together using the tip of a knife. Bake at 425° for 15 minutes. Reduce oven temperature to 250°; bake 45 minutes or until almost set. Let cool completely on a wire rack. Garnish with chocolate syrup and fresh raspberries, if desired. Yield: 12 servings.

POINTS: 6; **Exchanges:** 3 Starch, 1 Fat
Per serving: CAL 277 (24% from fat); PRO 7.9g; FAT 7.5g (sat 3.8g); CARB 44.1g; FIB 1.3g; CHOL 18mg; IRON 1.6mg; SOD 338mg; CALC 76mg

Gingered Apricot Crumble

Crystallized or candied ginger (found labeled both ways) is usually sold in jars in the spice section.

⅔ cup all-purpose flour
½ cup firmly packed brown sugar
1 teaspoon ground cinnamon
¼ teaspoon ground nutmeg
¼ cup chilled stick margarine, cut into small pieces
2 pounds fresh apricots, halved and pitted (about 12 large)
¾ cup firmly packed brown sugar
1 tablespoon chopped crystallized ginger
1 teaspoon vanilla extract
Cooking spray
2¼ cups vanilla low-fat ice cream

1. Preheat oven to 375°.

2. Combine first 4 ingredients in a medium bowl; cut in margarine with a pastry blender or 2

---

40 minutes or until mixture thickens slightly.

3. Beat egg whites and cream of tartar with clean, dry beaters at high speed of a mixer until foamy. Gradually add 2 tablespoons sugar, 1 tablespoon at a time, beating until stiff peaks form. Gently fold raspberry mixture into egg white mixture. Pour into prepared crust; chill 2 hours or until firm. Garnish with raspberries and mint, if desired. Yield: 8 servings.

POINTS: 3; **Exchanges:** 1 Starch, 1 Fat, ½ Fruit
Per serving: CAL 168 (35% from fat); PRO 3.6g; FAT 6.5g (sat 0.6g); CARB 24.4g; FIB 2.4g; CHOL 68mg; IRON 0.7mg; SOD 185mg; CALC 33mg

Brownie Cheese Pie

1 (15.1-ounce) package low-fat fudge brownie mix
1 (4-ounce) jar carrot baby food
2 teaspoons instant coffee granules
½ teaspoon ground cinnamon
Cooking spray
½ cup plus 2 tablespoons sugar, divided
4 teaspoons all-purpose flour
1 teaspoon vanilla extract
1 (8-ounce) package Neufchâtel cheese or light cream cheese, softened
1 (8-ounce) block fat-free cream cheese, softened

knives until mixture resembles coarse meal. Set mixture aside.

3. Combine apricots, ¾ cup brown sugar, ginger, and vanilla in a 9-inch square baking dish coated with cooking spray; toss well.

4. Sprinkle flour mixture evenly over apricots. Bake at 375° for 45 minutes or until apricot mixture is bubbly and topping is browned. Serve with ice cream. Yield: 9 servings (serving size: ½ cup apricot mixture and ¼ cup ice cream).

POINTS: 6; **Exchanges:** 2 Starch, 1½ Fruit, 1 Fat
Per serving: CAL 293 (22% from fat); PRO 3.5g; FAT 7g (sat 1.9g); CARB 56.3g; FIB 2.4g; CHOL 5mg; IRON 1.8mg; SOD 101mg; CALC 94mg

Peach-and-Blueberry Cobbler

Top this fruit-filled dessert with a dollop of vanilla low-fat frozen yogurt.

1   cup low-fat biscuit and baking mix
½   cup regular oats
¼   cup firmly packed brown sugar
½   teaspoon ground cinnamon
¼   cup chilled reduced-calorie stick margarine, cut into small pieces
4   cups frozen sliced peaches
2   cups frozen blueberries
¼   cup granulated sugar

1. Preheat oven to 350°.

2. Combine first 4 ingredients in a bowl; cut in margarine with a pastry blender or 2 knives until mixture resembles coarse meal. Set aside.

3. Combine peaches and blueberries in a 2-quart casserole; sprinkle with ¼ cup sugar. Sprinkle oat mixture evenly over fruit. Bake at 350° for 45 minutes or until bubbly. Yield: 6 servings (serving size: 1 cup).

POINTS: 5; **Exchanges:** 3 Starch, 1 Fruit, ½ Fat
Per serving: CAL 282 (19% from fat); PROTEIN 3.9g; FAT 6g (sat 1.1g); CARB 60.6g; FIB 3.7g; CHOL 0mg; IRON 1.5mg; SOD 417mg; CALC 19mg

Cherry Ping

Tap the top crust with a finger; if you hear it "ping," it's done. Canned cherries make Cherry Ping a dessert possibility year-round.

½   cup granulated sugar
¼   cup all-purpose flour

¼   cup whole-wheat flour
1   teaspoon baking powder
1   teaspoon vanilla extract
1   large egg, lightly beaten
2   (16-ounce) cans pitted tart red cherries in water, undrained
⅓   cup granulated sugar
1½ tablespoons cornstarch
⅛   teaspoon ground nutmeg
2   teaspoons lemon juice
⅛   teaspoon almond extract
1   teaspoon sifted powdered sugar

1. Preheat oven to 375°.

2. Combine first 4 ingredients in a medium bowl, and stir well. Add vanilla and egg, stirring until moist; set aside.

3. Drain cherries, reserving ½ cup liquid. Place cherries in an 8-inch square baking dish, and set aside. Combine ⅓ cup granulated sugar, cornstarch, and nutmeg in a medium bowl. Gradually add reserved cherry liquid, lemon juice, and almond extract, stirring with a whisk until mixture is blended. Pour juice mixture over cherries. Drop flour mixture by heaping teaspoons onto cherry mixture. Bake at 375° for 40 minutes or until top sounds hollow when tapped. Let cool

If you feel dinner's not over until you've had dessert, this Peach-and-Blueberry Cobbler is a quick-and-easy one. And it uses ingredients that are often on hand.

Rich chocolate filling and a tall, stately meringue will make Chocolate Meringue Pie a favorite in your home.

1. Combine flour and salt; cut in shortening with a pastry blender or 2 knives until mixture resembles coarse meal. Combine ice water and lemon juice. Add ice water mixture, 1 tablespoon at a time, to flour mixture, tossing with a fork until dry ingredients are moist. Gently press dough into a 4-inch circle on heavy-duty plastic wrap; cover with additional plastic wrap. Roll dough, still covered, into an 11-inch circle, and chill for 10 minutes or until plastic wrap can be easily removed.

2. Preheat oven to 425°.

3. Remove plastic wrap; fit dough into a 9-inch pie plate coated with cooking spray. Fold edges under and flute; pierce bottom and sides of dough with a fork. Bake at 425° for 14 minutes or until lightly browned; set aside on a wire rack. Reduce oven temperature to 325°.

4. Place 1 egg in a bowl; stir well, and set aside. Combine ½ cup sugar, cocoa, and 3 tablespoons plus 2 teaspoons cornstarch in a medium saucepan. Gradually add milk, stirring with a whisk until well blended. Bring mixture to a boil over medium heat, and cook 1 minute, stirring constantly. Gradually stir about one-fourth of hot cocoa mixture into egg, and add to remaining hot cocoa mixture, stirring constantly. Cook an additional 1 minute or until thick and bubbly, stirring constantly. Remove from heat, and stir in vanilla. Pour into prepared crust; cover surface of filling with plastic wrap, and set aside.

5. Beat 4 egg whites, remaining 1 teaspoon cornstarch, and cream of tartar at high speed of a mixer until foamy. Gradually add ⅓ cup sugar, 1 tablespoon at a time, beating until stiff peaks form (do not overbeat).

6. Uncover pie; spread meringue evenly over hot filling, sealing to edge of pastry. Bake at 325° for 25 minutes, and let cool 1 hour on a wire rack. Chill pie 3 hours or until set. Yield: 8 servings.

POINTS: 5; **Exchanges**: 2½ Starch, 1Fat
Per serving: CAL 246 (22% from fat); PRO 7g; FAT 5.9g (sat 2.1g); CARB 40.6g; FIB 0.5g; CHOL 29mg; IRON 1.4mg; SOD 112mg; CALC 87mg

20 minutes on a wire rack, and sprinkle with powdered sugar. Yield: 4 servings (serving size: 1 cup).

POINTS: 6; **Exchanges**: 1½ Fruit, 3½ Starch
Per serving: CAL 335 (5% from fat); PRO 5.2g; FAT 1.8g (sat 0.5g); CARB 77.5g; FIB 3.5g; CHOL 55mg; IRON 4.1mg; SOD 156mg; CALC 104mg

Chocolate Meringue Pie

1   cup all-purpose flour
⅛   teaspoon salt
3   tablespoons vegetable shortening
3   tablespoons plus 1 teaspoon ice water
1   teaspoon lemon juice
Cooking spray
1   large egg, lightly beaten
½   cup sugar
¼   cup plus 1 tablespoon cocoa
¼   cup cornstarch, divided
2   cups 1% low-fat milk
2   teaspoons vanilla extract
4   large egg whites (at room temperature)
¼   teaspoon cream of tartar
⅓   cup sugar

Apple-Cranberry Crumble

3   cups chopped Rome apple (about 4 large
    apples)
2   cups fresh cranberries
Cooking spray
½   cup granulated sugar
⅓   cup all-purpose flour
¼   cup firmly packed brown sugar
3   tablespoons reduced-calorie stick
    margarine, softened
1   cup regular oats
¼   cup chopped pecans
2   cups vanilla fat-free frozen yogurt

1. Preheat oven to 375°.

2. Layer apple and cranberries in an 8-inch
square baking dish coated with cooking spray;
sprinkle with granulated sugar.

3. Combine flour and brown sugar; cut in margarine with a pastry blender or 2 knives until
mixture resembles coarse meal. Stir in oats and
pecans. Sprinkle over fruit.

4. Bake at 375° for 25 minutes or until bubbly.
Let stand 5 minutes. Divide evenly between each
of 8 dessert dishes; top each with ¼ cup frozen
yogurt. Yield: 8 servings.

POINTS: 5; **Exchanges:** 2 Starch, 1 Fruit, 1 Fat
Per serving: CAL 255 (22% from fat); PRO 4.2g; FAT 6.2g (sat
0.5g); CARB 48.4g; FIB 3g; CHOL 0mg; IRON 1mg; SOD 73mg;
CALC 78mg

Cranberry-Chocolate Crumble

¾   cup water
½   cup granulated sugar
1   (12-ounce) bag fresh or frozen cranberries,
    thawed
⅓   cup seedless raspberry jam
Cooking spray
2   tablespoons milk chocolate chips
½   cup all-purpose flour
⅓   cup regular oats
¼   cup firmly packed brown sugar
3   tablespoons margarine, melted

1. Preheat oven to 350°.

2. Combine first 3 ingredients in a medium
saucepan; bring to a boil. Reduce heat, and simmer 10 minutes, stirring occasionally. Remove
from heat; stir in jam. Divide mixture evenly
among 6 (6-ounce) custard cups coated with

cooking spray, and sprinkle with chocolate chips.

3. Combine flour and next 3 ingredients; toss well.
Sprinkle oat mixture evenly over cranberry mixture. Place cups on a baking sheet; bake at 350°
for 20 minutes or until bubbly. Yield: 6 servings.

POINTS: 6; **Exchanges:** 3½ Starch, 1 Fat, ½ Fruit
Per serving: CAL 305 (22% from fat); PRO 2.5g; FAT 7.6g (sat 2g);
CARB 58.6g; FIB 1.5g; CHOL 2mg; IRON 1mg; SOD 82mg; CALC
19mg

Apple Slump With Nutmeg Sauce

¾   cup plus 1 tablespoon all-purpose flour
2   tablespoons sugar
1   tablespoon stick margarine, melted
¾   teaspoon baking powder
¼   teaspoon baking soda
⅛   teaspoon salt
⅓   cup low-fat buttermilk
4   cups peeled, thinly sliced cooking apple
    (about 1 pound)
¼   cup water
¼   cup thawed apple juice concentrate
½   teaspoon ground cinnamon
Nutmeg Sauce

1. Combine first 6 ingredients in a bowl; stir well.
Add buttermilk, stirring just until dry ingredients
are moist. Set aside.

2. Combine apple and next 3 ingredients in a
Dutch oven. Cover and cook over medium heat 5
minutes. Drop dough by tablespoons onto apple
mixture. Cover, reduce heat, and simmer 30 minutes (do not uncover Dutch oven during cooking
time).

3. Serve warm with Nutmeg Sauce. Yield: 4 servings (serving size: 1 cup apple mixture and ¼ cup
Nutmeg Sauce).

POINTS: 6; **Exchanges:** 2 Fruit, 2 Starch, ½ Fat
Per serving: CAL 299 (15% from fat); PRO 3.9g; FAT 4.9g (sat
0.9g); CARB 61.7g; FIB 3g; CHOL 0mg; IRON 2mg; SOD 343mg;
CALC 99mg

Nutmeg Sauce:

1   tablespoon all-purpose flour
1   tablespoon brown sugar
1   cup apple juice
1   teaspoon stick margarine
¼   teaspoon ground nutmeg
Dash of salt

■ THE NAME GAME

In many cases, there are several names for the same dessert. The name varies by the area of the country, which probably has something to do with the national-ity of the region's settlers.

■ **Cobblers** are basi-cally deep-dish pies with a biscuit-type top-ping. They are baked rather than cooked on the stove.

■ A **pandowdy** is fruit baked in a pan and topped with a crust. When the crust is lightly browned, it is cut up and pressed into the fruit and juices. This process is called "dowdying."

■ A **crisp** is a baked dessert with sugared and spiced fruit topped with a buttered (or toasted) crumb mix-ture. It is sometimes called a crumble in New England, Pennsylvania, or the Midwest. But in the Pacific Northwest, the same dessert is known as a buckle.

(continued on page 35)

1. Combine flour and brown sugar in a saucepan; stir well. Gradually add apple juice; stir well. Bring to a boil over medium heat. Add margarine, and cook 5 minutes. Remove from heat. Add nutmeg and salt; stir with a whisk until well blended. Yield: 1 cup.

Banana Cream Pie

To make gingersnap crumbs, use a food processor, or place the cookies in a zip-top plastic bag and crush with a rolling pin.

1¼ cups gingersnap crumbs (about 25 cookies)
2 tablespoons sugar
½ teaspoon ground cinnamon
1 large egg white, lightly beaten
1 tablespoon stick margarine, melted
Cooking spray
½ cup sugar
2 tablespoons cornstarch
¼ teaspoon salt
1 large egg
1 cup 1% low-fat milk
1 tablespoon stick margarine
2 teaspoons vanilla extract
2 cups sliced banana
1½ cups frozen reduced-calorie whipped topping, thawed
8 semisweet chocolate curls (optional)

1. Preheat oven to 325°.

2. Combine first 3 ingredients in a small bowl; stir well. Add 1 tablespoon of egg white (discard remaining egg white) and 1 tablespoon melted margarine; toss with a fork until moist. Press mixture into bottom and up sides of a 9-inch pie plate coated with cooking spray. Bake at 325° for 20 minutes; let cool on a wire rack.

3. Combine ½ cup sugar, cornstarch, salt, and 1 egg in a large bowl, and stir well with a whisk. Set mixture aside.

4. Heat milk over medium-high heat in a medium heavy saucepan to 180° or until tiny bubbles form around edge (do not boil). Remove from heat. Gradually add hot milk to sugar mixture, stirring constantly with whisk. Return milk mixture to pan. Add 1 tablespoon margarine, and cook over medium heat 4 minutes or until thick and bubbly, stirring constantly. Reduce heat to low, and cook an additional 2 minutes, stirring constantly. Remove from heat; stir in vanilla. Place pan in a large ice-filled bowl for 25 minutes or until egg mixture cools to room temperature, stirring occasionally.

5. Remove pan from ice. Fold in sliced banana, and spoon mixture into prepared crust. Spread whipped topping evenly over filling, and top with chocolate curls, if desired. Cover loosely, and chill 4 hours. Yield: 8 servings.

POINTS: 6; Exchanges: 2 Starch, 1 Fat, ½ Fruit
Per serving: CAL 253 (31% from fat); PRO 3.9g; FAT 8.9g (sat 2.2g); CARB 40.8g; FIB 1.2g; CHOL 34mg; IRON 1.1mg; SOD 161mg; CALC 81mg

Blackberry Cobbler

Fat-free yogurt in the biscuit topping is the key to making this light version of a summer favorite.

5 cups fresh blackberries (about 1¾ pounds)
¾ cup sugar
2 tablespoons all-purpose flour
1 teaspoon grated lemon rind
1 tablespoon fresh lemon juice
1 teaspoon vanilla extract
Cooking spray
1 cup all-purpose flour
½ teaspoon baking powder
½ teaspoon baking soda
½ cup vanilla fat-free yogurt
2 tablespoons fresh lemon juice
2 tablespoons stick margarine, melted
1 teaspoon vanilla extract
2 large egg whites

1. Preheat oven to 400°.

2. Combine first 6 ingredients; stir gently. Spoon blackberry mixture into an 11- x 7-inch baking dish coated with cooking spray; set aside.

3. Combine 1 cup flour, baking powder, and baking soda in a large bowl; stir well, and set aside. Combine yogurt and next 4 ingredients, and add to dry ingredients, stirring just until moist. Drop dough by tablespoons onto blackberry mixture.

4. Bake at 400° for 30 minutes or until filling is

Banana Cream Pie

bubbly and crust is golden. Serve warm. Yield: 8 servings (serving size: ¾ cup).

POINTS: 3; Exchanges: 2 Starch, 1 Fruit
Per serving: CAL 227 (14% from fat); PRO 4.2g; FAT 3.5g (sat 0.6g); CARB 45.7g; FIB 7.1g; CHOL 0mg; IRON 1.4mg; SOD 128mg; CALC 85mg

Maple-Pecan Tart

1   cup all-purpose flour
1   teaspoon sugar
¼   teaspoon salt
3   tablespoons vegetable shortening
3½ tablespoons ice water
Cooking spray
1   cup low-fat granola without raisins
1   cup maple syrup
2   teaspoons vanilla extract
⅛   teaspoon salt
3   large egg whites
1   large egg
⅓   cup chopped pecans

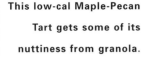

This low-cal Maple-Pecan Tart gets some of its nuttiness from granola.

1. Preheat oven to 450°.

2. Combine first 3 ingredients in a bowl; cut in shortening with a pastry blender or 2 knives until crumbly. Add ice water, 1 tablespoon at a time; toss with a fork until dry ingredients are moist.

3. Gently press mixture into a 4-inch circle on heavy-duty plastic wrap, and cover with additional plastic wrap. Roll dough, still covered, into an 11-inch circle, and chill for 10 minutes or until plastic wrap can be easily removed.

4. Remove plastic wrap; fit dough into a 9-inch round removable-bottom tart pan coated with cooking spray.

5. Break up any large pieces of granola, and sprinkle into pastry shell.

6. Combine maple syrup and next 4 ingredients, stirring with a whisk. Pour over granola, and sprinkle with pecans. Place on baking sheet.

7. Bake at 450° for 10 minutes. Reduce oven temperature to 325°, and bake 20 minutes. Let cool completely on a wire rack. Yield: 8 servings.

POINTS: 6; Exchanges: 3 Starch, 1 Fat
Per serving: CAL 286 (28% from fat); PRO 5g; FAT 8.9g (sat 1.7g); CARB 48.7g; FIB 1.4g; CHOL 28mg; IRON 3mg; SOD 153mg; CALC 39mg

Honey-Rhubarb Crumble

5½ cups (½-inch) sliced fresh rhubarb (about 1½ pounds)
¼   cup honey
1   teaspoon grated lime rind
Cooking spray
⅓   cup regular oats
⅓   cup all-purpose flour
¼   cup firmly packed brown sugar
3   tablespoons chilled stick margarine, cut into small pieces
1½ cups vanilla fat-free frozen yogurt

1. Preheat oven to 375°.

2. Combine rhubarb, honey, and grated lime rind in a bowl, and toss well. Spoon into an 8-inch square baking dish coated with cooking spray.

3. Place oats, flour, and brown sugar in a food processor, and pulse 2 to 3 times. Add chilled margarine, and process until mixture resembles coarse meal. Sprinkle over rhubarb mixture. Bake at 375° for 40 minutes or until rhubarb is tender.

Serve with frozen yogurt. Yield: 6 servings (serving size: ½ cup rhubarb mixture and ¼ cup frozen yogurt).

POINTS: 5; **Exchanges**: 2½ Starch, 1 Veg, ½ Fat
Per serving: CAL 237 (24% from fat); PRO 4.2g; FAT 6.4g (sat 1.2g); CARB 43.4g; FIB 1.3g; CHOL 0mg; IRON 1mg; SOD 107mg; CALC 178mg

Double-Chocolate Cream Tart

To complement the intensity of the filling and crust in this Double-Chocolate Cream Tart, we added a light whipped topping.

1   cup all-purpose flour, divided
¼   cup ice water
1   tablespoon vanilla extract, divided
¾   cup Dutch process or unsweetened cocoa, divided
2   tablespoons sugar
¼   teaspoon salt
¼   cup vegetable shortening
Cooking spray
1   (14-ounce) can fat-free sweetened condensed skim milk
6   ounces Neufchâtel cheese or light cream cheese (about ⅔ cup), softened
1   large egg
1   large egg white
1½ cups frozen reduced-calorie whipped topping, thawed
1   ounce semisweet chocolate, finely chopped

1. Combine ¼ cup flour, ice water, and 1 teaspoon vanilla, stirring with a whisk until well blended; set aside. Combine ¾ cup flour, ¼ cup cocoa, sugar, and salt in a bowl; cut in shortening with a pastry blender or 2 knives until mixture resembles coarse meal. Add ice water mixture; toss with a fork until moist and crumbly (do not form a ball). Gently press mixture into a 4-inch circle on heavy-duty plastic wrap; cover with additional plastic wrap. Roll dough, still covered, into a 13-inch circle. Chill dough 30 minutes or until plastic wrap can be easily removed.

2. Preheat oven to 350°.

3. Remove plastic wrap; fit dough into a 10-inch round removable-bottom tart pan coated with cooking spray. Fold edges under, and flute. Pierce bottom and sides of dough with a fork; bake at 350° for 4 minutes. Let cool on a wire rack. Place tart pan on a baking sheet; set aside.

4. Beat remaining ½ cup cocoa and milk at medium speed of a mixer until blended. Add cheese; beat well. Add remaining 2 teaspoons vanilla, egg, and egg white; beat just until smooth. Pour mixture into crust; bake at 350° for 25 minutes or until set (do not overbake). Let cool completely on a wire rack.

5. Spread whipped topping over tart; sprinkle with chopped chocolate. Store lightly covered in refrigerator. Yield: 12 servings.

POINTS: 6; **Exchanges**: 2½ Starch, 1½ Fat
Per serving: CAL 266 (33% from fat); PRO 7.8g; FAT 9.7g (sat 3.8g); CARB 36.1g; FIB 0.3g; CHOL 32mg; IRON 1.5mg; SOD 161mg; CALC 94mg

Blueberry Grunt

¾   cup all-purpose flour
¼   cup plus 2 tablespoons sugar, divided
1   teaspoon baking powder
¼   teaspoon salt
3   tablespoons chilled stick margarine, cut into small pieces

Serve Honey-Rhubarb Crumble in the spring when rhubarb is in season. Other times of the year, substitute frozen peaches, blueberries, or strawberries.

Dried-Fruit Cobbler With Molasses Biscuits

1½ cups water
1   cup orange juice
⅓   cup orange marmalade
2   (8-ounce) bags mixed dried fruit, coarsely chopped
1   cup all-purpose flour
1   teaspoon baking powder
¼   teaspoon ground cinnamon
⅛   teaspoon baking soda
Dash of ground cloves
⅓   cup chilled stick margarine, cut into small pieces
2   tablespoons skim milk
2   tablespoons molasses
1   tablespoon orange marmalade
2   teaspoons water

1. Preheat oven to 400°.

2. Combine 1½ cups water, orange juice, ⅓ cup orange marmalade, and dried fruit in a 2-quart baking dish; stir well. Bake at 400° for 30 minutes.

3. Combine flour, baking powder, cinnamon, baking soda, and ground cloves in a bowl, and cut in margarine with a pastry blender or 2 knives until mixture resembles coarse meal. Combine skim milk and molasses, and add to flour mixture, stirring just until dry ingredients are moist.

4. Turn dough out onto a lightly floured surface, and knead 5 or 6 times. Roll dough to ½-inch thickness, and cut with a 2-inch biscuit cutter into 10 biscuits. Remove fruit mixture from oven, and arrange biscuits on top of hot fruit mixture. Bake an additional 20 minutes or until biscuits are golden.

5. Combine 1 tablespoon orange marmalade and 2 teaspoons water in a bowl, and brush mixture over biscuits. Serve warm. Yield: 10 servings (serving size: ½ cup fruit mixture and 1 biscuit).

POINTS: 6; **Exchanges:** 2 Fruit, 1½ Starch, 1 Fat
Per serving: CAL 276 (20% from fat); PRO 2.4g; FAT 6.2g (sat 1.2g); CARB 55.6g; FIB 0.4g; CHOL 0mg; IRON 2.3mg; SOD 106mg; CALC 67mg

Steamed dumplings sit atop cooked, sweet blueberries in Blueberry Grunt.

3   tablespoons skim milk
3   cups fresh blueberries
1½ cups water
1   tablespoon lemon juice
⅛   teaspoon salt
⅛   teaspoon grated lemon rind
Dash of ground cinnamon

1. Combine flour, 2 tablespoons sugar, baking powder, and ¼ teaspoon salt; cut in margarine with a pastry blender or 2 knives until mixture resembles coarse meal. Add milk, 1 tablespoon at a time, tossing with a fork until moist (dough will be sticky). Set aside.

2. Combine remaining ¼ cup sugar, blueberries, and next 5 ingredients in a Dutch oven; stir well, and bring to a boil. Reduce heat, and simmer, uncovered, 5 minutes. Drop dough by tablespoons onto blueberry mixture; cook 10 minutes. Cover and cook an additional 10 minutes (do not uncover during cooking time). Serve warm. Yield: 4 servings (serving size: about 1 cup).

POINTS: 6; **Exchanges:** 2½ Starch, 1 Fruit, 1 Fat
Per serving: CAL 301 (28% from fat); PRO 3.6g; FAT 9.2g (sat 1.8g); CARB 53.3g; FIB 3.6g; CHOL 0mg; IRON 1.4mg; SOD 455mg; CALC 96mg

Sweet Potato-Bourbon Tart

2   tablespoons granulated sugar
2   tablespoons stick margarine
¼   teaspoon salt
1   ounce block-style fat-free cream cheese
     (about 4 teaspoons)
1   teaspoon vanilla extract
1   large egg
1¼ cups all-purpose flour
4   medium sweet potatoes (about 2¼
     pounds)
¾   cup firmly packed brown sugar
3   tablespoons bourbon or ¼ teaspoon rum
     extract and 3 tablespoons water
2   tablespoons stick margarine
2   teaspoons vanilla extract
½   teaspoon ground cinnamon
¼   teaspoon salt
¼   teaspoon ground nutmeg
¼   teaspoon ground allspice
2   large eggs
Cooking spray
2   teaspoons water
1   large egg white, lightly beaten
¼   cup chopped pecans

1. Preheat oven to 400°.
2. Combine first 4 ingredients in a medium bowl; beat at medium speed of a mixer until light and creamy. Add vanilla and 1 egg; beat well. Gradually add flour, beating at low speed until moist. Press mixture gently into a 5-inch circle on heavy-duty plastic wrap; cover with additional plastic wrap. Chill 1 hour.
3. Bake sweet potatoes at 400° for 55 minutes or until very tender. Let cool. Reduce oven temperature to 350°. Peel potatoes; place potato pulp, brown sugar, and next 8 ingredients in a large bowl. Beat at medium speed of mixer until smooth; set aside.
4. Roll dough, still covered, into an 11-inch circle. Remove plastic wrap, and fit dough into a 9-inch round removable-bottom tart pan coated with cooking spray. Spoon potato mixture into prepared crust. Combine 2 teaspoons water and egg white, and stir well. Brush edges of dough with egg white mixture. Sprinkle pecans over tart. Bake at 350° for 1 hour or until puffy and set.

Let cool on a wire rack. Yield: 10 servings.

POINTS: 6; **Exchanges:** 3 Starch, 1 Fat
Per serving: CAL 267 (29% from fat); PRO 5.3g; FAT 8.5g (sat 1.6g); CARB 42.2g; FIB 2g; CHOL 67mg; IRON 1.6mg; SOD 225mg; CALC 47mg

Chocolate-Mint Ice Cream Pie

½   cup evaporated skim milk
2   tablespoons unsweetened cocoa
2   tablespoons light-colored corn syrup
1   teaspoon cornstarch
¼   cup green crème de menthe, divided
1½ teaspoons vanilla extract, divided
3   (1-ounce) squares semisweet chocolate
2   tablespoons reduced-calorie stick
     margarine
1¼ cups oven-toasted rice cereal (such as Rice
     Krispies)
2   pints vanilla low-fat ice cream, softened
Chocolate curls (optional)

1. Combine first 4 ingredients in a small saucepan; place over medium heat, and bring to a boil, stirring constantly. Add 1 tablespoon crème de menthe; cook an additional 1 minute. Remove from heat; stir in ½ teaspoon vanilla. Let cool.
2. Line a 9-inch pie plate with foil, and fold excess foil under edge of pie plate.
3. Melt chocolate and margarine in a large heavy saucepan over low heat. Add 1 tablespoon crème de menthe; cook 1 minute, stirring constantly. Remove from heat; stir in cereal and remaining 1 teaspoon vanilla. Spread cereal mixture over bottom and up sides of prepared pie plate. Freeze 20 minutes or until firm; remove pie crust from pie plate, and discard foil. Return pie crust to pie plate, and return to freezer.
4. Combine ice cream and remaining 2 tablespoons crème de menthe, and stir well. Spread half of ice cream mixture in crust; freeze 30 minutes. Top with cocoa mixture, and freeze 10 minutes. Spread remaining ice cream mixture over cocoa mixture; cover and freeze at least 8 hours. Let pie stand 5 minutes before serving. Garnish with chocolate curls, if desired. Yield: 10 servings.

(continued from page 29)

■ A slump is fruit cooked in a pot on the stove with dumplings steamed on top. The name probably comes from the fact that the dish "slumps" on the plate. Louisa May Alcott, author of *Little Women*, named her Massachusetts home "Apple Slump."

■ A grunt is like a slump, but apparently it's mostly made with berries simmering in a skillet or saucepan with dumplings steamed on top. In Colonial times, the dessert was cooked in a kettle hung on a crane over an open fire. As the fruit cooked, it bubbled up and made gurgling or grunting noises.

POINTS: 4; **Exchanges:** 1½ Starch, 1 Fat, ½ Sk Milk
Per serving: CAL 177 (31% from fat); PRO 4.2g; FAT 6.1g (sat 3g); CARB 27.8g; FIB 0.9g; CHOL 9mg; IRON 0.4mg; SOD 65mg; CALC 125mg

Butterscotch Cream Pie

1   cup all-purpose flour
⅛   teaspoon salt
3   tablespoons vegetable shortening
3   tablespoons plus 2 teaspoons ice water
Cooking spray
⅔   cup firmly packed dark brown sugar
⅔   cup all-purpose flour
⅛   teaspoon salt
2   cups 1% low-fat milk
1   large egg yolk
2   teaspoons stick margarine
1½ teaspoons vanilla extract
½   cup frozen reduced-calorie whipped
      topping, thawed
2   teaspoons dark brown sugar

1. Preheat oven to 425°.

2. Combine 1 cup flour and ⅛ teaspoon salt in a bowl, and cut in shortening with a pastry blender or 2 knives until mixture resembles coarse meal. Add ice water, 1 tablespoon at a time, tossing with a fork until moist. Press mixture gently into a 4-inch circle on heavy-duty plastic wrap, and cover with additional plastic wrap. Roll dough, still covered, into an 11-inch circle, and chill for 10 minutes or until plastic wrap can be easily removed.

3. Remove plastic wrap; fit dough into a 9-inch pie plate coated with cooking spray. Fold edges under, and flute; pierce bottom and sides of dough with a fork. Bake at 425° for 15 minutes; let cool on a wire rack.

4. Combine ⅔ cup brown sugar, ⅔ cup flour, and ⅛ teaspoon salt in a medium saucepan. Gradually add milk and egg yolk, stirring with a whisk until well blended. Place over medium heat, and cook 16 minutes or until thick and bubbly, stirring constantly. Remove from heat; stir in margarine and vanilla. Pour mixture into prepared crust; cover surface of filling with plastic wrap. Chill 4 hours or until set.

5. Dollop whipped topping onto each serving; sprinkle 2 teaspoons brown sugar evenly over dollops. Yield: 8 servings.

POINTS: 5; **Exchanges:** 2½ Starch, 1 Fat
Per serving: CAL 250 (26% from fat); PRO 5g; FAT 7.1g (sat 2.3g); CARB 41.3g; FIB 0.7g; CHOL 30mg; IRON 1.9mg; SOD 122mg; CALC 102mg

Pumpkin-Praline Pie

Because this pie is so festive, double the recipe and make two—then give one as a gift.

1   cup all-purpose flour, divided
3½ tablespoons ice water
1   teaspoon granulated sugar
¼   teaspoon salt
3   tablespoons vegetable shortening
Cooking spray
1¾ cups unsweetened canned pumpkin
1   cup 2% reduced-fat milk
½   cup firmly packed brown sugar
1   tablespoon all-purpose flour
3   tablespoons maple syrup
2   tablespoons bourbon
½   teaspoon salt
1½ teaspoons ground cinnamon
1½ teaspoons vanilla extract
¼   teaspoon ground ginger
¼   teaspoon ground nutmeg
¼   teaspoon ground allspice
2   large egg whites, lightly beaten
1   large egg, lightly beaten
⅓   cup coarsely chopped pecans
¼   cup firmly packed brown sugar
1½ teaspoons dark corn syrup
½   teaspoon vanilla extract

1. Preheat oven to 400°.

2. Combine ¼ cup flour and ice water, stirring with a whisk until well blended; set aside. Combine remaining ¾ cup flour, granulated sugar, and ¼ teaspoon salt in a bowl; cut in shortening with a pastry blender or 2 knives until mixture resembles coarse meal. Add ice water mixture; toss with a fork until dry ingredients are moist. Gently press mixture into a 4-inch circle on heavy-duty plastic wrap, and cover with additional plastic wrap. Roll dough, still covered, into an 11-inch circle, and chill for 10 minutes or until plastic wrap can be easily removed.

3. Remove plastic wrap; fit dough into a 9-inch pie plate coated with cooking spray. Fold edges under, and flute; pierce bottom and sides of dough with a fork. Bake at 400° for 15 minutes; let cool on a wire rack.

4. Combine canned pumpkin and next 13 ingredients in a bowl, and stir well with a whisk. Pour into prepared piecrust, and bake at 400° for 40 minutes.

5. Combine chopped pecans, ¼ cup brown sugar, corn syrup, and ½ teaspoon vanilla, and stir well. Sprinkle pecan mixture over pie, and bake an additional 15 minutes or until filling is set (shield edges of piecrust with foil, if necessary). Let pie cool completely on a wire rack. Yield: 8 servings.

POINTS: 6; **Exchanges:** 3 Starch, 1 Fat, ½ Veg
Per serving: CAL 292 (28% from fat); PRO 5.4g; FAT 9g (sat 2.1g); CARB 46.3g; FIB 3.1g; CHOL 30mg; IRON 2.4mg; SOD 270mg; CALC 89mg

Cherry Cobbler

1   tablespoon cornstarch
1   tablespoon lemon juice
8   cups pitted fresh cherries
    (about 3 pounds)
3   tablespoons plus 1 teaspoon sugar, divided
6   tablespoons water
¼   teaspoon ground cinnamon
¼   teaspoon almond extract
1   cup all-purpose flour
¼   teaspoon salt
¼   teaspoon ground nutmeg
¼   cup chilled stick margarine, cut into small pieces and chilled
3   tablespoons plus 1 teaspoon ice water
Fresh sweet cherry with stem (optional)

1. Preheat oven to 425°.

2. Combine cornstarch and lemon juice in a large Dutch oven, and stir well. Add pitted fresh cherries, 3 tablespoons sugar, water, and cinnamon, and stir gently. Bring to a boil over medium heat, and cook 1 minute or until mixture is thick.

3. Remove from heat; stir in almond extract.

Spoon cherry mixture into an 8-inch square baking dish; set aside.

4. Combine flour, salt, and nutmeg, and cut in margarine with a pastry blender or 2 knives until mixture resembles coarse meal. Add ice water, 1 tablespoon at a time, tossing with a fork until moist. Gently press mixture into a 4-inch square on heavy-duty plastic wrap; cover with additional plastic wrap. Roll dough, still covered, into an 8- x 9-inch rectangle, and chill for 10 minutes or until plastic wrap can be easily removed.

5. Remove plastic wrap; cut dough into 16 (½-inch-wide) strips. Arrange pastry strips lattice-style over cherry mixture. Sprinkle with remaining 1 teaspoon sugar. Bake at 425° for 25 minutes or until filling is bubbly and pastry is golden. Garnish with a fresh cherry, if desired. Serve warm. Yield: 10 servings (serving size: ¾ cup).

POINTS: 4; **Exchanges:** 1½ Fruit, 1 Starch, 1 Fat
Per serving: CAL 198 (27% from fat); PRO 3g; FAT 5.9g (sat 1.2g); CARB 35.7g; FIB 3g; CHOL 0mg; IRON 0.9mg; SOD 112mg; CALC 23mg

Pumpkin-Praline Pie is two classic American pies in one: pumpkin and pecan—what a combo.

Stacked in Your Favor

WHEN YOU HAVE PLACES TO GO
AND PEOPLE TO SEE,
YOU CAN'T BEAT COOKIES.

Most of us consider the cookie a child's dessert. But kids don't take advantage of its greatest asset: its portability. They sit down to an afterschool snack of cookies and milk, they raid the cookie jar, ruining their appetite for dinner, but they never take their cookies anywhere. That's unfortunate, especially when you consider that the word "cookie" comes from the Dutch "koekje," which means "little cakes"—little cakes you can snack on at your desk, munch on while you walk the dog, or serve easily on the back patio. Brownies and bars offer the same advantages, which is why this no-utensils-needed dessert is so popular. And it follows that whether you nibble on Giant Gingersnaps or Fudgy Cream Cheese Brownies there are no dishes to wash.

Oatmeal-Raisin Cookies—just like Grandma's, but with only 2 POINTS.

Oatmeal-Raisin Cookies

¾ cup firmly packed brown sugar
⅓ cup stick margarine, softened
¼ cup granulated sugar
1 large egg
⅓ cup skim milk
1 teaspoon vanilla extract
1½ cups all-purpose flour
¾ teaspoon baking soda
½ teaspoon ground cinnamon
¼ teaspoon salt
¼ teaspoon ground nutmeg
1½ cups quick-cooking oats
¾ cup raisins
Cooking spray

1. Preheat oven to 375°.

2. Beat first 3 ingredients in a large bowl at medium speed of a mixer until blended. Add egg, and beat well. Add milk and vanilla; beat well.

3. Combine flour and next 4 ingredients; gradually add to sugar mixture, beating well. Stir in oats and raisins.

4. Drop dough by level tablespoons onto baking sheets coated with cooking spray. Bake at 375° for 9 minutes or until lightly browned. Remove cookies from pans; let cool on wire racks. Yield: 3½ dozen (serving size: 1 cookie).

POINTS: 2; **Exchanges:** 1 Starch
Per serving: CAL 76 (24% from fat); PRO 1.7g; FAT 2g (sat 0.4g); CARB 13g; FIB 0.2g; CHOL 4mg; IRON 0.6mg; SOD 57mg; CALC 11mg

Banana-Macadamia Madeleines

These French cakes require a madeleine pan, which has shell-shaped cups. The pans can be purchased in cookware stores.

1 cup mashed ripe banana
1 tablespoon stick margarine, melted
2 teaspoons dark rum or ⅛ teaspoon imitation rum extract
1 teaspoon vanilla extract
4 large egg whites
¾ cup plus 2 tablespoons sifted powdered sugar
¾ cup sifted cake flour
1 teaspoon baking powder
¼ teaspoon salt
⅓ cup macadamia nuts, toasted and chopped
Baking spray with flour
2 tablespoons powdered sugar

1. Preheat oven to 375°.

2. Place mashed banana in a food processor, and process until smooth. Add margarine, dark rum, vanilla, and egg whites; process until mixture is blended. Combine ¾ cup plus 2 tablespoons powdered sugar, flour, baking powder, and salt; add to food processor, and pulse 2 to 3 times or until blended. Add chopped nuts, and pulse 2 times or until well blended.

3. Spoon 1 tablespoon batter into each of 12 madeleine molds coated with baking spray. Bake at 375° for 15 minutes or until puffy. Remove from pan immediately, and let cool on a wire rack. Repeat procedure with remaining batter. Sift 2 tablespoons powdered sugar over madeleines. Yield: 2½ dozen (serving size: 1 madeleine).

POINTS: 1; **Exchanges:** ½ Starch, ½ Fat
Per serving: CAL 53 (27% from fat); PRO 0.9g; FAT 1.6g (sat 0.3g); CARB 9g; FIB 0.3g; CHOL 0mg; IRON 0.3mg; SOD 31mg; CALC 11mg

White Chocolate Chip Cookies

⅔ cup granulated sugar
⅔ cup firmly packed brown sugar
¼ cup plus 3 tablespoons stick margarine, softened
¼ cup skim milk
1 teaspoon vanilla extract
¼ teaspoon butter extract
2 large eggs
3½ cups all-purpose flour
1½ teaspoons baking soda
½ teaspoon salt
⅔ cup vanilla-flavored milk chips
Cooking spray

1. Preheat oven to 350°.

2. Combine first 7 ingredients in a large bowl; beat at medium speed of a mixer until blended. Combine flour, baking soda, and salt; add to margarine mixture, beating well. Stir in vanilla-flavored chips.

3. Drop dough by rounded tablespoons 2 inches apart onto baking sheets coated with cooking spray. Bake at 350° for 12 minutes. Remove

Banana-Macadamia Madeleines:

These delicate sponge-cake cookies go well with coffee.

Dip Soft Spice Biscotti in coffee or milk, or just enjoy them by themselves.

375° for 25 minutes. Remove rectangles from baking sheet; let cool 10 minutes on a wire rack. Cut each rectangle diagonally into (¾-inch) slices. Yield: 2 dozen (serving size: 1 cookie).

POINTS: 2; **Exchanges:** 1 Starch, ½ Fat
Per serving: CAL 98 (28% from fat); PRO 1.5g; FAT 3g (sat 0.5g); CARB 16.6g; FIB 0.4g; CHOL 6mg; IRON 1mg; SOD 7mg; CALC

Thumbprint Cookies

1   (17.5-ounce) package chocolate chip cookie mix
1   cup regular oats
⅓   cup water
1   teaspoon vanilla extract
1   large egg white
Cooking spray
¼   cup plus 2 teaspoons strawberry jam

1. Preheat oven to 375°.

2. Combine first 5 ingredients in a medium bowl, and stir well. Drop dough by rounded teaspoons 1 inch apart onto baking sheets coated with cooking spray.

3. Press center of each cookie with thumb, making an indentation; fill with ¼ teaspoon jam. Bake at 375° for 10 minutes or until golden. Remove cookies from pans; let cool on wire racks. Store in an airtight container. Yield: 4½ dozen (serving size: 1 cookie).

POINTS: 1; **Exchanges:** ½ Starch, ½ Fat
Per serving: CAL 55 (33% from fat); PRO 0.8g; FAT 2.0g (sat 1g); CARB 8.5g; FIB 0.2g; CHOL 0mg; IRON 0.2mg; SOD 34mg; CALC 1mg

cookies from pans; let cool on wire racks. Yield: 4½ dozen (serving size: 1 cookie).

POINTS: 2; **Exchanges:** 1 Starch
Per serving: CAL 82 (29% from fat); PRO 1.2g; FAT 2.6g (sat 1.1g); CARB 13.1g; FIB 0.2g; CHOL 8mg; IRON 0.5mg; SOD 82mg; CALC 6mg

Soft Spice Biscotti

Unlike regular crunchy biscotti that are baked twice, these cookies are only baked once and have a much softer texture.

1   cup granulated sugar
1   cup firmly packed dark brown sugar
½   cup sliced almonds
⅓   cup vegetable oil
2   teaspoons ground cinnamon
1   teaspoon ground cloves
2   teaspoons water
2   large egg whites
1   large egg
2½ cups all-purpose flour
2   teaspoons baking powder
Cooking spray

1. Preheat oven to 375°.

2. Combine first 9 ingredients in a large bowl, and beat at low speed of a mixer for 1 minute. Combine flour and baking powder; gradually add flour mixture to sugar mixture, beating until well blended (dough will be soft). Turn dough out onto a lightly floured surface, and shape dough into 3 (6- x 4-inch) rectangles. Place rectangles on a baking sheet coated with cooking spray, and flatten to ¾-inch thickness. Bake at

Cappuccino Crinkles

Use your microwave oven to melt the marshmallows. That way, you won't have to stir the marshmallows as they melt, and they're less likely to burn.

1   tablespoon instant coffee granules
1   tablespoon hot water
1   teaspoon vanilla extract
1   (10-ounce) package marshmallows
5   cups crisp rice cereal (such as Rice Krispies)
Cooking spray

1. Combine first 3 ingredients in a small bowl, stirring until coffee dissolves.

2. Place marshmallows in a 2-quart glass measure, and microwave at HIGH 1½ to 2 minutes or until marshmallows melt. Stir until mixture is smooth. Add coffee mixture to melted marshmallows, and stir well. Working quickly, add crisp rice cereal to marshmallow mixture, stirring gently to coat. Press mixture into a 13- x 9-inch baking pan coated with cooking spray. Let cool completely. Cut into bars. Yield: 24 bars (serving size: 1 bar).

POINTS: 1; **Exchanges:** 1 Starch
Per serving: CAL 63 (1% from fat); PRO 0.6g; FAT 0.1g (sat 0.0g); CARB 14.9g; FIB 0.1g; CHOL 0mg; IRON 0.4mg; SOD 49mg; CALC 2mg

Almond Chess Squares

1   (18.25-ounce) package light yellow cake mix
1   (8-ounce) block fat-free cream cheese, softened
2½ cups sifted powdered sugar
½   cup reduced-calorie stick margarine, melted
1   tablespoon water
1½ teaspoons almond extract
1   teaspoon butter extract
3   large egg whites
1   large egg
Cooking spray
2   teaspoons powdered sugar

1. Preheat oven to 350°.

2. Combine first 9 ingredients in a large bowl; beat at medium speed of a mixer until smooth. Pour batter into a 13- x 9-inch baking pan coated with cooking spray. Bake at 350° for 45 minutes or until golden. Let cool completely in pan on a wire rack. Sift 2 teaspoons powdered sugar over cookies. Cut into bars. Yield: 3 dozen (serving size: 1 bar).

POINTS: 3; **Exchanges:** 1½ Starch
Per serving: CAL 117 (19% from fat); PRO 2.3g; FAT 2.5g (sat 0.6g); CARB 20.2g; FIB 0g; CHOL 7mg; IRON 0.3mg; SOD 205mg; CALC 32mg

Sweet Cornmeal Cookies

Remove the cookies from the baking sheets before they cool. They will crumble if you let them cool on the pans.

⅔   cup firmly packed brown sugar
½   cup all-purpose flour
2   tablespoons cornmeal
Dash of salt
¼   cup stick margarine, melted
2   large egg whites, lightly beaten
Cooking spray

1. Combine brown sugar, all-purpose flour, cornmeal, and salt in a medium bowl, and stir well. Add melted margarine and egg whites, and stir well. Cover and let stand 1 hour (batter will be thin).

2. Preheat oven to 400°.

3. Spoon batter by level teaspoons 2 inches apart onto baking sheets coated with cooking spray. Bake at 400° for 5 minutes or until edges are browned. Let cookies cool on pans 1 minute. Remove cookies from pans, and let cool completely on wire racks. Yield: 44 cookies (serving size: 2 cookies).

POINTS: 1; **Exchanges:** ½ Starch, ½ Fat
Per serving: CAL 58 (34% from fat); PRO 0.6g; FAT 2.2g (sat 0.4g); CARB 9.2g; FIB 0.2g; CHOL 0mg; IRON 0.2mg; SOD 19mg; CALC 6mg

With the help of a cake mix, Almond Chess Squares go from mixing bowl to oven in minutes.

Lemon Squares pack
a mouthwatering
burst of flavor.

Lemon Squares

1 cup all-purpose flour
⅓ cup sifted powdered sugar
⅓ cup chilled stick margarine, cut into small pieces
Cooking spray
1 cup granulated sugar
1½ teaspoons grated lemon rind
½ cup fresh lemon juice
2 tablespoons all-purpose flour
½ teaspoon baking powder
¼ teaspoon salt
¼ teaspoon butter extract
3 large egg whites
1 large egg
2 tablespoons powdered sugar

1. Preheat oven to 350°.

2. Combine 1 cup flour and ⅓ cup powdered sugar; cut in margarine with a pastry blender or 2 knives until mixture is crumbly. Press firmly into bottom of an 11- x 7-inch baking dish coated with cooking spray. Bake at 350° for 20 minutes or until lightly browned.

3. Combine granulated sugar and next 8 ingredients; stir with a whisk until blended, and pour over crust. Bake at 350° for 20 minutes or until set. Let cool on a wire rack. Cut into squares, and sift 2 tablespoons powdered sugar over cookies. Yield: 2 dozen (serving size: 1 square).

POINTS: 2; **Exchanges**: 1 Starch, ½ Fat
Per serving: CAL 92 (27% from fat); PRO 1.3g; FAT 2.8g (sat 0.6g); CARB 15.7g; FIB 0.2g; CHOL 9mg; IRON 0.3mg; SOD 74mg; CALC 9mg

Benne Seed Wafers

½ cup firmly packed brown sugar
5 tablespoons stick margarine, melted
⅔ cup all-purpose flour
2 tablespoons sesame seeds, toasted
2 tablespoons water
Dash of salt
1 large egg white, lightly beaten

1. Preheat oven to 400°.

2. Cover a baking sheet with parchment paper, and set aside.

3. Combine brown sugar and margarine in a bowl; stir well. Add remaining ingredients; stir until

well blended. Spoon batter by level teaspoons 3 inches apart onto prepared baking sheet. Using the back of a spoon, spread batter into 2-inch circles. Bake at 400° for 6 minutes or until edges are lightly browned; let cool on pan 1 minute. Remove wafers from paper; let cool completely on wire racks. Yield: 4 dozen (serving size: 2 wafers).

Note: You can reuse the same piece of parchment paper for each batch you bake.

POINTS: 1; **Exchanges**: ½ Starch, ½ Fat
Per serving: CAL 56 (45% from fat); PRO 0.6g; FAT 2.8g (sat 0.6g); CARB 7.4g; FIB 0.2g; CHOL 0mg; IRON 0.4mg; SOD 32mg; CALC 12mg

Molasses-Spice Crackles

1⅓ cups all-purpose flour
1 teaspoon baking soda
½ teaspoon ground ginger
½ teaspoon ground cinnamon
¼ teaspoon salt
¼ teaspoon ground cloves
½ cup firmly packed brown sugar
¼ cup stick margarine, softened
2 tablespoons molasses
1 large egg white
¼ cup granulated sugar

1. Combine first 6 ingredients in a bowl; stir well, and set aside.

2. Place brown sugar, margarine, molasses, and egg white in a food processor, and process until blended. Add flour mixture; process until blended, scraping sides of processor bowl once. Gently press mixture into a ball; wrap in plastic wrap. Chill 2 hours.

3. Preheat oven to 375°.

4. Shape dough into 40 (¾-inch) balls. Place granulated sugar in a bowl. Dip balls in cold water; shake to remove excess moisture. Roll wet balls in sugar. Place 3 inches apart on a baking sheet. Bake at 375° for 10 minutes. Remove cookies from pans; let cool on wire racks. Yield: 40 cookies (serving size: 1 cookie).

POINTS: 1; **Exchanges**: ½ Starch
Per serving: CAL 40 (27% from fat); PRO 0.5g; FAT 1.2g (sat 0.2g); CARB 6.9g; FIB 0.1g; CHOL 0mg; IRON 0.3mg; SOD 62mg; CALC 5mg

LIGHT COOKIE FORMULA

Making light cookies is a lot like conducting a science experiment—the right balance of ingredients is crucial. So if you're inclined to change or vary the ingredients, be careful. Here are our tips for making great cookies.

■ **If the batter seems dry and you're tempted to add more liquid, don't. This makes for a cakelike cookie that spreads too much.**

■ **Always use stick margarine instead of the kind in a tub. Also, be careful not to use low-fat margarine or anything that's labeled "spread."**

■ **Too much flour will make low-fat cookies dry and crumbly. To measure flour correctly, stir the flour, and then lightly spoon (don't pack) it into a dry measuring cup, leveling it off with the flat side of a knife. Do not tap or shake measuring cup.**

■ **If the dough is too soft to shape or roll, simply chill until slightly firm.**

Easy Peanut Butter Cookies

1⅔ cups all-purpose flour
1½ tablespoons cornstarch
1¾ teaspoons baking powder
½ teaspoon baking soda
¾ cup firmly packed brown sugar
¼ cup granulated sugar
¼ cup vegetable oil
¼ cup creamy peanut butter
1½ tablespoons light-colored corn syrup
2½ teaspoons vanilla extract
1 large egg
Cooking spray
3 tablespoons granulated sugar

1. Preheat oven to 375°.

2. Combine all-purpose flour, cornstarch, baking powder, and baking soda in a medium bowl; stir well, and set mixture aside. Combine brown sugar, ¼ cup granulated sugar, vegetable oil, and peanut butter in a large bowl; beat at medium speed of a mixer until mixture is well blended. Add corn syrup, vanilla, and egg; beat well. Stir in flour mixture.

3. Coat hands lightly with cooking spray, and shape dough into 48 (1-inch) balls. Roll balls in 3 tablespoons granulated sugar, and place 2 inches apart on baking sheets coated with cooking spray. Flatten balls with the bottom of a glass.

4. Bake at 375° for 7 minutes or until cookies are lightly browned. Remove from pans, and let cookies cool on wire racks. Yield: 4 dozen (serving size: 1 cookie).

POINTS: 1; **Exchanges:** ½ Starch, ½ Fat
Per serving: CAL 59 (31% from fat); PRO 1g; FAT 2g (sat 0.4g); CARB 9.5g; FIB 0.2g; CHOL 5mg; IRON 0.3mg; SOD 23mg; CALC 14mg

Fudgy Cream Cheese Brownies

¾ cup sugar
6 tablespoons reduced-calorie stick margarine, softened
1 large egg
1 large egg white
1 tablespoon vanilla extract
½ cup all-purpose flour
¼ cup unsweetened cocoa
Cooking spray

1 (8-ounce) tub light cream cheese, softened
¼ cup sugar
1 large egg white

1. Preheat oven to 350°.

2. Beat ¾ cup sugar and margarine at medium speed of a mixer until light and fluffy. Add egg, 1 egg white, and vanilla, and beat well. Add flour and cocoa, and beat well. Pour batter into a 9-inch square baking pan coated with cooking spray, and set aside.

3. Beat cream cheese and ¼ cup sugar at high speed of a mixer until smooth. Add 1 egg white; beat well. Dollop cream cheese mixture over chocolate mixture, and swirl together using the tip of a knife.

4. Bake at 350° for 27 minutes or until done (do not overcook). Let cool completely on a wire rack. Cut into squares. Yield: 16 brownies (serving size: 1 brownie).

POINTS: 3; **Exchanges:** 1 Starch, 1 Fat
Per serving: CAL 136 (39% from fat); PRO 2.8g; FAT 5.9g (sat 1.6g); CARB 17g; FIB 0.1g; CHOL 23mg; IRON 0.3mg; SOD 120mg; CALC 26mg

Apple-Spice Bars

Leave the peel on the apples for added color.

1 cup all-purpose flour
½ cup whole-wheat flour
1 teaspoon baking soda
1 teaspoon ground cinnamon
¼ teaspoon salt
¼ teaspoon ground cloves
¼ cup reduced-calorie stick margarine, softened
½ cup firmly packed brown sugar
1 cup unsweetened applesauce
1 teaspoon vanilla extract
1 cup finely chopped cooking apples
1 cup dried currants
½ cup regular oats
⅓ cup butterscotch chips
Cooking spray

1. Preheat oven to 350°.

2. Combine first 6 ingredients; stir well, and set aside. Beat margarine at medium speed of a mixer

Ribbons of sweet, creamy cheese flow through Fudgy Cream Cheese Brownies.

Did you ever wonder where vanilla comes from? Its source is a wrinkled brown bean, the product of a climbing orchid native to southeastern Mexico. The beans grow between 4 and 12 inches in length; after harvest, they go through a fermentation-and-drying process for four to six months. During this time, they turn from light to dark brown as they shrivel into the pencil-thin, brownish-black vanilla beans that we buy encased in glass tubes; they also develop their characteristic sweet aroma.

The prize inside each vanilla bean is a rich, concentrated paste—the pure essence of vanilla. This paste is actually made up of thousands of tiny dot-like seeds.

REMOVING SEEDS FROM A VANILLA BEAN

1 Using a small knife with a sharp tip, cut vanilla beans in half lengthwise.

2 Scrape seeds out with knife blade, or push seeds out of vanilla bean half with thumbnail.

until creamy. Add brown sugar, beating until light and fluffy. Add flour mixture to margarine mixture alternately with applesauce, beginning and ending with flour mixture. Stir in vanilla. Stir in chopped apple and next 3 ingredients. Pour batter into an 11- x 7-inch baking dish coated with cooking spray.

3. Bake at 350° for 40 minutes or until a wooden pick inserted in center comes out clean. Let cool in pan on a wire rack. Cut into bars. Yield: 2 dozen (serving size: 1 bar).

POINTS: 2; **Exchanges:** 1 Starch, ½ Fat
Per serving: CAL 92 (19% from fat); PRO 1.4g; FAT 1.9g (sat 0.5g); CARB 18.2g; FIB 0.9g; CHOL 0mg; IRON 0.8mg; SOD 101mg; CALC 17mg

Snappy Almond Stars

Carefully measuring the flour is critical in this recipe. For optimal snap and crunch, roll the dough out as thin as possible.

½ cup firmly packed dark brown sugar
¼ cup light butter (such as Land O' Lakes)
1 tablespoon cold water
1 cup plus 2 tablespoons all-purpose flour
2 tablespoons cornstarch
½ teaspoon ground cinnamon
⅛ teaspoon salt
¼ cup sliced almonds

1. Beat brown sugar and butter at medium speed of a mixer until well blended (about 5 minutes). Add water, and beat well. Combine flour, cornstarch, cinnamon, and salt; add to sugar mixture, beating until well blended. Gently press dough into a 4-inch disk, and wrap in plastic wrap. Freeze 30 minutes.

2. Preheat oven to 375°.

3. Remove plastic wrap. Roll dough to a ¹⁄₁₆-inch thickness on a lightly floured surface; cut with a 2-inch star-shaped cookie cutter. Place cookies on a baking sheet; sprinkle almonds evenly over cookies. Bake at 375° for 8 minutes or until cookies are crisp and edges are browned. Let cool on pan 30 seconds. Remove cookies from pan,

and let cool on wire racks. Yield: 4 dozen (serving size: 2 cookies).

POINTS: 1; **Exchanges:** ½ Starch
Per serving: CAL 25 (29% from fat); PRO 0.4g; FAT 0.8g (sat 0.4g); CARB 4.1g; FIB 0.1g; CHOL 5mg; IRON 0.2mg; SOD 13mg; CALC 3mg

Vanilla Wafers

Look for vanilla beans in the spice section.

Cooking spray
1 tablespoon all-purpose flour
½ cup sugar
¼ cup cornstarch
2 tablespoons stick margarine, melted
1 large egg
1 (6-inch) vanilla bean, split lengthwise
¾ cup all-purpose flour
½ teaspoon baking powder
⅛ teaspoon salt

1. Preheat oven to 350°.

2. Coat 2 large baking sheets with cooking spray, and dust with 1 tablespoon flour; set aside.

3. Combine sugar and next 3 ingredients in a large bowl; stir well with a whisk. Scrape seeds from vanilla bean; add seeds to sugar mixture, reserving bean for another use. Add ¾ cup flour, baking powder, and salt; stir until smooth.

4. Drop dough by rounded teaspoons 2 inches apart onto prepared baking sheets. Bake at 350° for 15 minutes. Remove cookies from pans, and let cool on wire racks. Yield: 3 dozen (serving size: 2 cookies).

POINTS: 1; **Exchanges:** ½ Starch, ½ Fat
Per serving: CAL 32 (23% from fat); PRO 0.5g; FAT 0.8g (sat 0.2g); CARB 5.6g; FIB 0.1g; CHOL 6mg; IRON 0.2mg; SOD 17mg; CALC 4mg

Double-Chocolate Chews

1¾ cups all-purpose flour
⅔ cup sifted powdered sugar
⅓ cup unsweetened cocoa
2¼ teaspoons baking powder
⅛ teaspoon salt
1 cup semisweet chocolate mini chips, divided
3 tablespoons vegetable oil
1 cup firmly packed brown sugar
2½ tablespoons light-colored corn syrup

1 tablespoon water
2½ teaspoons vanilla extract
3 large egg whites
Cooking spray

1. Preheat oven to 350°.

2. Combine first 5 ingredients in a bowl; stir well, and set aside.

3. Combine ¾ cup chocolate chips and vegetable oil in a small saucepan, and cook over low heat until chocolate melts, stirring constantly. Pour melted chocolate mixture into a large bowl, and let cool 5 minutes. Add brown sugar and next 4 ingredients to chocolate mixture, and stir well. Stir in flour mixture and remaining ¼ cup chocolate chips.

4. Drop dough by level tablespoons 2 inches apart onto baking sheets coated with cooking spray. Bake at 350° for 8 minutes. Let cool on pans 2 minutes or until firm. Remove cookies from pans; let cool on wire racks. Yield: 4 dozen (serving size: 1 cookie).

POINTS: 1; **Exchanges:** ½ Starch, ½ Fat
Per serving: CAL 64 (23% from fat); PRO 0.9g; FAT 1.6g (sat 0.6g); CARB 11.8g; FIB 0.1g; CHOL 0mg; IRON 0.5mg; SOD 13mg; CALC 19mg

Frosted Peppermint Brownies

¾ cup reduced-calorie stick margarine, softened
1⅓ cups sugar
½ cup fat-free sour cream
⅓ cup evaporated skim milk
1 teaspoon peppermint extract
8 large egg whites
1⅓ cups all-purpose flour
⅔ cup unsweetened cocoa
1 teaspoon baking powder
½ teaspoon salt
Cooking spray
Creamy Chocolate Frosting
3 tablespoons crushed peppermint candies (about 6 candies)

1. Preheat oven to 350°.

2. Cream margarine; gradually add sugar, beating at medium speed of a mixer until mixture is well blended. Add sour cream, evaporated milk, peppermint extract, and egg whites; beat well.

3. Combine flour and next 3 ingredients; stir well. Add flour mixture to margarine mixture, beating until blended. Pour batter into a 13- x 9-inch baking pan coated with cooking spray. Bake at 350° for 25 minutes or until a wooden pick inserted in center comes out clean. Let brownies cool completely in pan on a wire rack. Spread Creamy Chocolate Frosting over cooled brownies, and sprinkle with crushed peppermint candies. Cut into squares. Yield: 2 dozen (serving size: 1 brownie).

POINTS: 4; **Exchanges:** 2½ Starch
Per serving: CAL 191 (21% from fat); PRO 3.5g; FAT 4.2g (sat 0.2g); CARB 35.3g; FIB 0.2g; CHOL 0mg; IRON 0.9mg; SOD 158mg; CALC 28mg

Creamy Chocolate Frosting:

3 cups sifted powdered sugar
¼ cup unsweetened cocoa
¼ cup skim milk
2 teaspoons vanilla extract
¼ teaspoon salt

Friends and neighbors will appreciate a gift of Double-Chocolate Chews.

Try our lightened Hamantaschen. You won't believe it's low-fat.

1. Combine all ingredients in a medium bowl, and stir until frosting is spreading consistency. Yield: 1 cup.

Hamantaschen

Begin preparing this Purim favorite the day ahead so the dough and filling can chill overnight. (For more about the holiday, see the sidebar at right.)

⅔   cup sugar
6   tablespoons stick margarine
1   teaspoon vanilla extract
2   ounces block-style fat-free cream cheese
    (about ¼ cup)
1   large egg
2   cups all-purpose flour
1½ teaspoons baking powder
¼   teaspoon salt
12 ounces dried figs (about 2 cups)
3   tablespoons sugar
3   tablespoons boiling water
1   tablespoon light-colored corn syrup
1   tablespoon lemon juice
Cooking spray

1. Combine ⅔ cup sugar, margarine, vanilla, and cream cheese in a large bowl; beat at medium speed of a mixer 2 minutes or until light and fluffy. Add egg, and beat at high speed 1 minute or until mixture is very smooth. Combine flour, baking powder, and salt; add to sugar mixture, beating at low speed just until flour mixture is moist. Divide dough in half, and gently shape each portion into a ball. Wrap dough in plastic wrap, and chill 8 hours or overnight.

2. Place figs in a food processor; pulse 6 times or until chopped. With processor on, slowly add 3 tablespoons sugar, boiling water, corn syrup, and lemon juice through food chute; process until smooth, scraping sides of processor bowl twice. Spoon fig mixture into a bowl; cover and chill 8 hours or overnight.

3. Shape each ball of dough into a 10-inch log. Cut each log into 10 (1-inch) slices; place on a tray lined with wax paper. Chill 30 minutes.

4. Preheat oven to 400°.

5. Place each slice of dough between 2 sheets of wax paper, and flatten to a 3½-inch circle using a rolling pin. Spoon 1 level tablespoon fig mixture into the center of each circle. With floured hands, bring 3 sides of dough over fig filling to form a triangle, and pinch edges of dough together to seal. Place filled triangles 2 inches apart on baking sheets coated with cooking spray, and bake at 400° for 10 minutes or until pastries are lightly browned. Remove from pans, and let cool on wire racks. Yield: 20 pastries (serving size: 1 pastry).

POINTS: 3; **Exchanges:** 2 Starch
Per serving: CAL 163 (22% from fat); PRO 2.6g; FAT 4g (sat 0.8g); CARB 30.3g; FIB 3.2g; CHOL 12mg; IRON 1mg; SOD 93mg; CALC 57mg

No-Bake Fig Bars

The oats may be toasted in a skillet over medium-high heat or on a baking sheet in a 350° oven.

1½ cups chopped dried figs
1   tablespoon all-purpose flour
½   cup water

¾ cup sweetened flaked coconut
½ cup reduced-calorie stick margarine
¼ cup sugar
1¾ cups quick-cooking oats, toasted
½ teaspoon vanilla extract
Cooking spray

1. Combine chopped figs and flour; toss lightly to coat.

2. Bring water to a boil in a medium saucepan. Add fig mixture, coconut, margarine, and sugar; reduce heat to medium, and cook 5 minutes or until mixture is thick, stirring frequently. Add quick-cooking oats and vanilla, stirring until oats are moist.

3. Press mixture in bottom of a 9-inch square baking pan coated with cooking spray. Cover and chill. Cut into bars. Yield: 2 dozen (serving size: 1 bar).

POINTS: 2; **Exchanges:** 1 Starch, ½ Fat
Per serving: CAL 111 (41% from fat); PRO 1.5g; FAT 4.6g (sat 1.6g); CARB 15.3g; FIB 2.9g; CHOL 0mg; IRON 0.6mg; SOD 39mg; CALC 22mg

Peanut Butter-Oat Squares

Cut these bar cookies while they are warm. Once they cool, they tend to crumble when cut.

2 cups regular oats
1 cup crisp rice cereal (such as Rice Krispies)
⅓ cup firmly packed brown sugar
¼ cup light-colored corn syrup
2 tablespoons reduced-calorie stick margarine
¼ cup reduced-fat creamy peanut butter
½ teaspoon vanilla extract
Cooking spray

1. Preheat oven to 250°.

2. Combine oats and cereal in a large bowl; stir well, and set aside.

3. Combine brown sugar, corn syrup, and margarine in a saucepan; cook over medium-high heat until margarine melts, stirring constantly. Remove from heat; stir in peanut butter and vanilla. Pour over cereal mixture; stir well.

4. Press mixture firmly into an 8-inch square baking pan coated with cooking spray. Bake at 250°

for 45 minutes or until golden. Let cool in pan 10 minutes; cut into squares. Let cool completely in pan. Yield: 16 squares (serving size: 1 square).

POINTS: 2; **Exchanges:** 1 Starch
Per serving: CAL 87 (29% from fat); PRO 1.9g; FAT 2.8g (sat 0.4g); CARB 14.4g; FIB 0.2g; CHOL 0mg; IRON 1.2mg; SOD 46mg; CALC 15mg

Chocolate-Nut Popcorn Clusters

1½ cups sugar
½ cup water
⅓ cup light-colored corn syrup
2 tablespoons unsweetened cocoa
1 teaspoon vanilla extract
½ teaspoon baking soda
¼ teaspoon salt
7 cups popped corn (popped without salt or fat)
½ cup coarsely chopped unsalted dry-roasted peanuts
Cooking spray

1. Combine first 4 ingredients in a large Dutch oven; stir until smooth. Bring to a boil over medium-high heat, and cook to hard crack stage (310°), stirring occasionally. Remove from heat; stir in vanilla, baking soda, and salt. Add popped corn and peanuts. Working rapidly, toss mixture gently, and spread onto a baking sheet coated with cooking spray. Let cool; break into pieces. Store in an airtight container. Yield: 17 servings (serving size: 1 ounce).

POINTS: 3; **Exchanges:** 1½ Starch
Per serving: CAL 125 (17% from fat); PRO 1.6g; FAT 2.3g (sat 0.3g); CARB 25.3g; FIB 0.8g; CHOL 0mg; IRON 0.3mg; SOD 68mg; CALC 10mg

Giant Gingersnaps

1¾ cups plus 2 tablespoons all-purpose flour
¾ teaspoon ground ginger
½ teaspoon baking soda
½ teaspoon ground cinnamon
⅛ teaspoon ground cloves
Dash of salt
3 tablespoons stick margarine, softened
⅓ cup sugar
1 large egg white
2 tablespoons molasses

THE COOKIE HOLIDAY

Celebrated in late February or early March, Purim might as well be called the cookie holiday. Queen Esther is credited with saving the Jews from the wicked Haman, so haman-taschen—the three-cornered pastries said variously to represent Haman's ears, hat, or pockets—are the star attraction. Because Purim comes 40 days before Passover, kosher Jewish bakers use flour, yeast, and other leavenings as freely as they can.

1 tablespoon orange juice
2 teaspoons sugar
Cooking spray

1. Preheat oven to 350°.

2. Combine first 6 ingredients; stir well, and set mixture aside.

3. Cream margarine; gradually add ⅓ cup sugar, beating at medium speed of a mixer until well blended. Add egg white; beat well. Add molasses and orange juice; beat well. Gradually add flour mixture, beating until well blended.

4. Shape dough into 1-inch balls; roll balls in 2 teaspoons sugar. Place balls 4 inches apart on a baking sheet coated with cooking spray. Flatten balls into 3-inch circles with the bottom of a glass. Bake at 350° for 6 minutes or until browned. Let cool slightly on pans. Carefully remove cookies from pans; let cool completely on wire racks. Yield: 34 cookies (serving size: 1 cookie).

POINTS: 1; **Exchanges:** ½ Starch
Per serving: CAL 47 (21% from fat); PRO 0.8g; FAT 1.1g (sat 0.2g); CARB 8.6g; FIB 0.2g; CHOL 0mg; IRON 0.4mg; SOD 37mg; CALC 4mg

Basic Icebox Sugar Cookies

1 cup all-purpose flour
¼ teaspoon baking soda
⅛ teaspoon salt
4 tablespoons stick margarine, softened
⅔ cup sugar
1 teaspoon vanilla extract
1 large egg white
Cooking spray

1. Combine flour, baking soda, and salt; stir well, and set aside. Beat margarine at medium speed of a mixer until light and fluffy. Gradually add sugar, beating at medium speed of a mixer until well blended. Add vanilla and egg white, and beat well. Add flour mixture, and stir until well blended. Turn dough out onto wax paper, and shape into a 6-inch log. Wrap log in wax paper, and freeze for 3 hours or until very firm.

2. Preheat oven to 350°.

3. Cut log into 24 (¼-inch-thick) slices, and place slices 1 inch apart on a baking sheet coated with cooking spray. Bake at 350° for 8 minutes. Remove cookies from pans; let cool on wire racks. Yield: 2 dozen (serving size: 1 cookie).

POINTS: 1; **Exchanges:** ½ Starch, ½ Fat
Per serving: CAL 59 (31% from fat); PRO 0.7g; FAT 2g (sat 0.4g); CARB 9.6g; FIB 0.1g; CHOL 0mg; IRON 0.2mg; SOD 50mg; CALC 2mg

Chocolate-Pine Nut Meringue Smooches

These are traditionally served at Passover, when flourless desserts are the rule. The meringue can be very sensitive to humidity, so it's best not to make them on a damp day.

4 large egg whites (at room temperature)
⅛ teaspoon salt
¼ teaspoon cream of tartar
1 cup sugar
1 teaspoon vanilla extract
⅓ cup pine nuts, toasted
2 ounces bittersweet chocolate, finely chopped

1. Preheat oven to 250°.

2. Beat egg whites and salt with clean, dry beaters at medium speed of a mixer until foamy. Add cream of tartar, and beat until soft peaks form. Gradually add sugar, 2 tablespoons at a time, beating at medium-high speed until stiff peaks form. Add vanilla, and beat well. Fold in pine nuts and chocolate.

3. Cover a baking sheet with parchment paper. Spoon egg white mixture into 16 mounds on prepared baking sheet. Bake at 250° for 1 hour or until dry to touch (meringues are done when the surface is dry and they can be removed from paper without sticking to fingers). Turn oven off, and partially open oven door; leave meringues in oven 30 minutes. Remove from oven; carefully remove meringues from paper. Store meringues in an airtight container up to 3 days. Yield: 16 meringues (serving size: 1 meringue).

POINTS: 2; **Exchanges:** 1 Starch
Per serving: CAL 87 (28% from fat); PRO 1.8g; FAT 2.7g (sat 0.9g); CARB 15.3g; FIB 0.1g; CHOL 0mg; IRON 0.4mg; SOD 32mg; CALC 3mg

Chocolate-Pine Nut
Meringue Smooches:
A crispy shell encases a
nutty chocolate center.

Spoon Foods

PUT YOUR SPOON TO GOOD USE
WITH THESE CREAMY INDULGENCES.

Whoever invented the spoon was a genius. Think about it: The graceful curve of the bowl of the spoon is as beautiful as it is useful, but an empty spoon, while interesting, isn't as impressive as a spoon full of rich delicious dessert. Eating was, after all, undoubtedly the inventor's muse. Unfortunately, the poor guy never got to see his creation brimming with Butterscotch Tapioca or Crème Caramel, desserts with textures as tempting as their tastes. Once you've tasted the recipes in this chapter, we think you'll agree that a dessert spoon is what that culinary-minded caveman had in mind all along.

Use ripe bananas for a sweeter, more flavorful Banana Pudding.

speed of a mixer until foamy. Gradually add sugar, 1 tablespoon at a time, beating until stiff peaks form. Spread meringue evenly over pudding, sealing to edge of dish. Bake at 325° for 25 minutes or until golden. Yield: 10 servings (serving size: ¾ cup).

Note: Banana Pudding may be a bit soupy when you first remove it from the oven. Let it cool at least 30 minutes before serving.

POINTS: 7; **Exchanges:** 3½ Starch
Per serving: CAL 359 (10% from fat); PRO 7.9g; FAT 2.9g (sat 1g); CARB 49.5g; FIB 0.1g; CHOL 51mg; IRON 0.4mg; SOD 155mg; CALC 161mg

Steamed Chocolate Pudding With Brandied Cherry Sauce

1¾ cups all-purpose flour
2 teaspoons baking powder
½ teaspoon salt
1¼ cups semisweet chocolate chips
½ cup water
6 tablespoons unsweetened cocoa
2 tablespoons stick margarine
2 teaspoons instant coffee granules
¾ cup sugar
⅓ cup egg substitute
1 cup skim milk
½ teaspoon vanilla extract
Cooking spray
Brandied Cherry Sauce
Fresh cherries with stems (optional)

1. Sift first 3 ingredients together; set aside.

2. Combine chocolate chips and next 4 ingredients in a small saucepan; place over low heat, and cook 4 minutes or until mixture is smooth, stirring constantly. Let cool completely.

3. Combine sugar and egg substitute; beat at high speed of a mixer for 5 minutes. Add chocolate mixture; beat at low speed until blended. Add flour mixture alternately with milk, beginning and ending with flour mixture. Stir in vanilla.

4. Spoon into a 1½-quart steamed-pudding mold coated with cooking spray; cover tightly with foil or lid coated with cooking spray.

5. Place mold on a shallow rack in a stockpot; add boiling water to halfway up sides of mold. Cover

The dense texture of Steamed Chocolate Pudding With Brandied Cherry Sauce is typical of this old-fashioned dessert.

Banana Pudding

⅓ cup all-purpose flour
Dash of salt
2½ cups 1% low-fat milk
1 (14-ounce) can fat-free sweetened condensed skim milk
2 large egg yolks
2 teaspoons vanilla extract
3 cups sliced ripe banana, divided
45 reduced-fat vanilla wafers, divided
4 large egg whites (at room temperature)
¼ cup sugar

1. Preheat oven to 325°.

2. Combine flour and salt in a medium saucepan. Gradually add milks and yolks; stir well. Cook over medium heat 8 minutes or until thick, stirring constantly. Remove from heat; stir in vanilla.

3. Arrange 1 cup banana in bottom of a 2-quart baking dish. Spoon one-third of pudding mixture over banana. Arrange 15 wafers on top of pudding. Repeat layers twice, arranging the last 15 wafers around edge of dish. Push cookies into pudding.

4. Beat egg whites with clean, dry beaters at high

and cook in simmering water 1 hour or until knife inserted near center comes out clean, adding water to stockpot as needed.

6. Remove from water, and let pudding cool in mold on a wire rack for 15 minutes. Invert pudding onto a serving platter, and cut into 14 slices. Spoon warm Brandied Cherry Sauce on individual plates; place pudding slices on plates with sauce. Garnish with fresh cherries, if desired. Yield: 14 servings.

POINTS: 6; **Exchanges:** 3 Starch, ½ Fat
Per serving: CAL 257 (23% from fat); PRO 4.3g; FAT 6.5g (sat 3.1g); CARB 45.9g; FIB 0.6g; CHOL 4mg; IRON 1.5mg; SOD 196mg; CALC 83mg

Brandied Cherry Sauce:

2 cups frozen, pitted dark sweet cherries, thawed
⅓ cup water
⅓ cup sugar
¼ cup brandy
¼ cup water
1 tablespoon cornstarch

1. Place cherries and ⅓ cup water in a blender, and process until mixture is smooth. Strain purée, and discard pulp.

2. Combine cherry purée, sugar, and brandy in a small saucepan. Place over medium-high heat, and cook 1 minute or until sugar dissolves, stirring constantly. Bring mixture to a boil; reduce heat, and simmer 10 minutes, stirring occasionally. Combine ¼ cup water and cornstarch; stir until well blended. Add to cherry mixture; bring to a boil, and cook 1 minute or until slightly thick. Serve sauce warm with steamed pudding. Yield: 2 cups.

New England Corn Pudding With Maple Syrup Sauce

When you make this baked pudding, don't shortcut the leisurely cooking time. It takes a while for the flavors to develop.

1 large egg
3 cups 1% low-fat milk
½ cup water
½ cup yellow cornmeal
⅓ cup molasses
½ teaspoon ground ginger
⅛ teaspoon salt
1 tablespoon stick margarine
Cooking spray
Maple Syrup Sauce

1. Preheat oven to 300°.

2. Place egg in a bowl; stir well, and set aside. Combine milk and water in a 2-quart glass measure, and microwave at HIGH 7 minutes. Add cornmeal, and stir until mixture is blended. Microwave at HIGH 2 minutes, stirring after 1 minute. Stir one-fourth of cornmeal mixture into egg, and add to remaining cornmeal mixture, stirring constantly. Stir in molasses, ginger, and salt; microwave at HIGH 2 minutes, stirring after 1 minute. Add margarine, stirring until margarine melts.

3. Pour mixture into a 1½-quart casserole coated with cooking spray. Bake, uncovered, at 300° for 2½ hours or until set. Serve warm with Maple Syrup Sauce. Yield: 5 servings (serving size: 1 cup pudding and 2 tablespoons sauce).

POINTS: 6; **Exchanges:** 3½ Starch
Per serving: CAL 280 (17% from fat); PRO 7.3g; FAT 5.2g (sat 1.8g); CARB 51.7g; FIB 0.7g; CHOL 48mg; IRON 2.2mg; SOD 182mg; CALC 249mg

Maple Syrup Sauce:

¼ cup maple syrup
3 tablespoons brown sugar
1 tablespoon fresh lemon juice
¼ cup hot water

1. Combine first 3 ingredients in a heavy saucepan; place over medium heat. Cover and cook 5 minutes or until mixture boils and sugar dissolves. Uncover; cook an additional 5 minutes or until dark brown and very thick. Remove from heat, and carefully add hot water, stirring constantly. Serve warm. Yield: ⅔ cup.

Butterscotch Tapioca

4 cups skim milk
¼ cup uncooked quick-cooking tapioca

2 large eggs, lightly beaten
1 teaspoon vanilla extract
¼ cup stick margarine
⅔ cup firmly packed dark brown sugar

1. Combine first 3 ingredients in a medium saucepan; let stand 5 minutes. Bring to a boil over medium heat, and cook 35 minutes or until thick, stirring constantly. Remove from heat, and stir in vanilla.

2. Melt margarine in a small saucepan over medium heat. Add brown sugar, and cook 3 minutes, stirring constantly. Add to tapioca mixture; stir well. Pour into a bowl; cover surface of pudding with plastic wrap, and chill. Yield: 9 servings (serving size: ½ cup).

POINTS: 4; **Exchanges:** 1 Starch, 1 Fat, ½ Sk Milk
Per serving: CAL 177 (33% from fat); PRO 5.2g; FAT 6.4g (sat 1.5g); CARB 25g; FIB 0g; CHOL 47mg; IRON 0.8mg; SOD 135mg; CALC 156mg

Caramelized Sweet Potato Pudding

3 medium sweet potatoes (about 2 pounds)
½ cup sliced almonds
¾ cup sugar
Cooking spray
2 large egg whites (at room temperature)
¼ cup sugar
1 teaspoon vanilla extract

1. Preheat oven to 400°.

2. Wrap sweet potatoes in foil; bake at 400° for 1 hour or until tender. Let cool; peel potatoes.

3. Place sweet potatoes and almonds in a food processor; process until smooth. Spoon sweet potato mixture into a large nonstick skillet; keep warm over low heat.

4. Place ¾ cup sugar in a medium skillet; cook over medium-high heat 5 minutes or until sugar dissolves and turns golden. Immediately pour three-fourths of caramelized sugar into warm sweet potato mixture, stirring constantly. Set the remaining caramelized sugar aside.

5. Spoon sweet potato mixture into a 1½-quart casserole coated with cooking spray; set aside. Beat egg whites with clean, dry beaters at high speed of a mixer until foamy. Add sugar, 1 tablespoon at a time, beating until stiff peaks form. Add vanilla; beat well. Spread meringue evenly over warm sweet potato mixture, sealing to edge of dish. Bake at 400° for 15 minutes or until meringue is golden. Place remaining caramelized sugar over low heat until warm and melted (caramel will have hardened); drizzle over meringue. Serve warm. Yield: 8 servings (serving size: ¾ cup).

POINTS: 5; **Exchanges:** 3½ Starch
Per serving: CAL 257 (12% from fat); PRO 3.9g; FAT 3.5g (sat 0.4g); CARB 53.9g; FIB 4.1g; CHOL 0mg; IRON 0.9mg; SOD 29mg; CALC 40mg

Maple Rice Pudding

We used short-grain Arborio rice to create a richer, creamier texture.

4 cups 2% reduced-fat milk
⅔ cup Arborio rice or other short-grain rice
⅔ cup maple syrup
¼ cup raisins
1 teaspoon vanilla extract
¼ teaspoon salt
¼ teaspoon ground cinnamon
¼ teaspoon ground nutmeg

1. Combine first 4 ingredients in a medium saucepan; bring to a boil over medium heat, stir-

Caramelized Sweet Potato Pudding has a golden meringue topping.

ring frequently. Reduce heat to low, and cook 50 minutes or until rice is tender and mixture is creamy, stirring occasionally. Remove from heat; stir in remaining ingredients. Serve warm, at room temperature, or chilled. Yield: 8 servings.

POINTS: 4; **Exchanges:** 2½ Starch
Per serving: CAL 206 (11% from fat); PRO 5.3g; FAT 2.5g (sat 1.5g); CARB 40.6g; FIB 0.5g; CHOL 10mg; IRON 1.2mg; SOD 137mg; CALC 170mg

Lemon-Rosemary Custard Cakes

3   large egg whites (at room temperature)
¾   cup granulated sugar, divided
2   tablespoons stick margarine, softened
¼   cup all-purpose flour
1   teaspoon grated lemon rind
¼   cup fresh lemon juice
1   teaspoon minced fresh rosemary
Dash of salt
1½ cups 1% low-fat milk
3   large egg yolks
Cooking spray
1   tablespoon sifted powdered sugar
Rosemary sprigs (optional)

1. Preheat oven to 350°.
2. Beat egg whites with clean, dry beaters at medium-high speed of a mixer until foamy. Gradually add ¼ cup granulated sugar, 1 tablespoon at a time, beating until stiff peaks form. Set aside.
3. Beat remaining ½ cup granulated sugar and margarine at medium speed of a mixer until well blended (about 5 minutes). Add flour and next 4 ingredients; beat well. Add milk and egg yolks; beat well. Gently stir one-fourth of egg white mixture into batter; gently fold in remaining egg white mixture. Spoon into 6 (6-ounce) custard cups coated with cooking spray. Place cups in a baking pan; add hot water to pan to a depth of 1 inch. Bake at 350° for 45 minutes or until set. Remove cups from pan, and sprinkle powdered sugar evenly over each pudding. Garnish with rosemary sprigs, if desired. Yield: 6 servings.

POINTS: 5; **Exchanges:** 2½ Starch, 1 Fat
Per serving: CAL 222 (29% from fat); PRO 5.9g; FAT 7.2g (sat 2g); CARB 34.4g; FIB 0.2g; CHOL 113mg; IRON 0.7mg; SOD 113mg; CALC 92mg

Crème Caramel

½   cup sugar, divided
1   tablespoon water
Cooking spray
¼   cup amaretto
3   large eggs, lightly beaten
1½ cups 2% reduced-fat milk
½   cup evaporated skim milk
1½ teaspoons vanilla extract
¼   teaspoons almond extract

1. Preheat oven to 300°.
2. Combine ¼ cup sugar and water in a small heavy saucepan over medium heat; cook until sugar dissolves. Continue cooking an additional 8 minutes or until golden. Immediately pour into 6 (6-ounce) custard cups or ramekins coated with cooking spray, tipping quickly until sugar coats bottoms of cups; set aside.
3. Combine remaining ¼ cup sugar, amaretto, and eggs in a medium bowl; stir well with a whisk. Add milks and extracts; stir well. Pour mixture evenly into prepared cups; place cups in a large shallow pan. Add hot water to pan to a depth of 1 inch.
4. Bake at 300° for 1 hour and 10 minutes or

Fresh rosemary adds an unexpected kick to Lemon-Rosemary Custard Cakes.

**Summer Fruit With
Custard Sauce**

until a knife inserted near center comes out clean. Remove custard cups from water; let cool. Cover and chill 8 hours.

5. Loosen edges of custard with a spatula. Invert custards onto individual plates, and drizzle any remaining caramelized sugar evenly over custards. Yield: 6 servings.

POINTS: 3; **Exchanges:** 1½ Starch, ½ L-F Milk
Per serving: CAL 153 (22% from fat); PRO 6.8g; FAT 3.7g (sat 1.5g); CARB 22.5g; FIB 0g; CHOL 112mg; IRON 0.5mg; SOD 87mg; CALC 149mg

Summer Fruit With Custard Sauce

Stir Asti wine into the custard just before serving to give the sauce a sweet sparkle.

1⅔ cups 1% low-fat milk
⅔ cup sugar
1½ tablespoons cornstarch
1 large egg
1 large egg yolk
1 teaspoon vanilla extract
¾ cup Asti sparkling wine
1½ cup fresh raspberries
3 medium fresh peaches, each peeled and cut into 8 wedges

1. Heat milk over medium-high heat in a small heavy saucepan to 180° or until tiny bubbles form around edge of saucepan (do not boil). Remove from heat.

2. Combine sugar and cornstarch in a medium bowl; gradually add milk, stirring constantly with a whisk. Return milk mixture to saucepan, and cook over medium heat 4 minutes or until thick, stirring constantly.

3. Place egg and egg yolk in a bowl; stir well with a whisk. Gradually add hot milk mixture to egg, stirring constantly with whisk. Return milk mixture to pan; cook over medium-low heat 6 minutes or until thick, stirring constantly. Remove from heat. Pour sauce into a bowl; stir in vanilla. Cover surface of sauce with plastic wrap; let cool to room temperature. Chill thoroughly.

4. Stir sparkling wine into chilled sauce. Spoon sauce into dessert dishes; top with raspberries and peaches. Yield: 6 servings (serving size: ⅓ cup sauce, ¼ cup raspberries, and 4 peach slices)

Note: Substitute 24 frozen peach slices, thawed, if desired.

POINTS: 4 ; **Exchanges:** 2 Starch, ½ Fruit
Per serving: CAL 206(12% from fat); PRO 4.5g; FAT 2.7g (sat 1g); CARB 36.8g; FIB 3.1g; CHOL 76mg; IRON 0.7mg; SOD 48mg; CALC 102mg

Fig Bar Bread Pudding With Amaretto Sauce

7 cups cubed day-old French bread
8 fat-free fig fruit chewy cookies, crumbled
Cooking spray
1½ cups skim milk
½ cup granulated sugar
½ cup firmly packed brown sugar
1 tablespoon vanilla extract
½ teaspoon ground cinnamon
1 (12-ounce) can evaporated skim milk
1 (8-ounce) carton egg substitute
Amaretto Sauce

1. Preheat oven to 350°.

2. Combine bread and crumbled cookies in a 13- x 9-inch baking dish coated with cooking spray.

3. Combine skim milk and next 6 ingredients in a bowl; stir well. Pour over bread mixture; cover and chill 2 hours.

4. Uncover and bake at 350° for 45 minutes or until a knife inserted near center comes out clean. Serve with Amaretto Sauce. Yield: 10 servings (serving size: 1 piece of pudding and about 3 tablespoons sauce).

POINTS: 6; **Exchanges:** 4 Starch
Per serving: CAL 323 (6% from fat); PRO 9.3g; FAT 2.3g (sat 0.3g); CARB 64.6g; FIB 1.3g; CHOL 3mg; IRON 1.3mg; SOD 283mg; CALC 202mg

Amaretto Sauce:

½ cup sugar
½ cup amaretto-flavored liquid nondairy creamer
1 cup skim milk
2 tablespoons cornstarch

1. Combine sugar and nondairy creamer in a 2-quart glass measure or bowl. Microwave at HIGH 2 minutes or until sugar dissolves, stirring every 30 seconds. Combine milk and cornstarch; stir well. Add cornstarch mixture to creamer mixture; stir well. Microwave at HIGH 2 minutes or until thick and bubbly, stirring after 1 minute. Serve warm. Yield: 2 cups.

Sweet Potato Flan

To save time, substitute 1 cup of canned mashed sweet potato for the fresh sweet potato.

1   large sweet potato (about 1 pound)
½   cup sugar
2   (14-ounce) cans fat-free sweetened condensed skim milk
2½ cups egg substitute
2   cups skim milk
1   teaspoon ground cinnamon
1   teaspoon vanilla extract
½   teaspoon ground allspice
¼   teaspoon ground cloves
1   tablespoon flaked sweetened coconut, toasted

1. Preheat oven to 375°.

2. Pierce sweet potato several times with a fork; place on a baking sheet.

3. Bake at 375° for 1 hour or until done; let cool slightly. Peel sweet potato, and mash. Set aside 1 cup mashed sweet potato. Reserve remaining sweet potato for another use. Reduce oven temperature to 325°.

4. Sprinkle sugar in a 10-inch round cake pan. Place over medium heat, and cook until sugar melts and turns light golden brown, stirring constantly. Remove pan from heat, tipping quickly until caramelized sugar coats bottom of pan. Set aside. (Caramelized sugar will harden and may crack slightly as it cools.)

5. Combine 1 cup sweet potato, condensed milk, and next 6 ingredients; stir well. Pour half of mixture into a blender; process until smooth. Pour puréed mixture into a large bowl. Repeat procedure with remaining sweet potato mixture; pour into bowl, and stir well with a whisk. Pour mixture over caramelized sugar in cake pan. Cover with foil; place cake pan in a larger baking pan. Add hot water to larger pan to a depth of ½ inch.

6. Bake at 325° for 1 hour and 15 minutes or until a knife inserted near center comes out clean. Remove cake pan from water. Uncover and let cool on a wire rack 30 minutes.

7. Cover and chill at least 4 hours. Run a knife around edge of flan to loosen, and invert onto a serving platter. Sprinkle with toasted coconut. Yield: 16 servings.

POINTS: 4; **Exchanges:** 2½ Starch, ½ Sk Milk
Per serving: CAL 210 (1% from fat); PRO 9g; FAT 0.3g (sat 0.2g); CARB 43.1g; FIB 0.7g; CHOL 5.6mg; IRON 0.6mg; SOD 126mg; CALC 182mg

Vanilla Pudding

½   cup sugar
3   tablespoons cornstarch
⅛   teaspoon salt
2¼ cups 2% reduced-fat milk
1   large egg
1   teaspoon vanilla extract

1. Combine first 3 ingredients in a small saucepan; stir well. Combine milk and egg in a bowl; stir well with a whisk. Gradually add milk mixture to sugar mixture in pan, stirring constantly with whisk. Bring to a boil over medium heat, and cook 1 minute, stirring constantly. Remove from heat; stir in vanilla. Serve warm. Yield: 5 servings (serving size: ½ cup).

Sweet Potato Flan: The classic Spanish baked custard gets a makeover with the addition of sweet potato.

POINTS: 4; Exchanges: 1½ Starch, ½ L-F Milk
Per serving: CAL 168 (17% from fat); PRO 4.9g; FAT 3.1g (sat 1.6g); CARB 29.9g; FIB 0g; CHOL 51mg; IRON 0.2mg; SOD 127mg; CALC 139mg

Sweet Kugel

1 cup 1% low-fat cottage cheese
¾ cup raisins
½ cup sugar
2 tablespoons reduced-calorie stick margarine, melted
1 teaspoon ground cinnamon
¼ teaspoon salt
1 (16-ounce) can unsweetened sliced peaches in juice, drained and coarsely chopped
4 (8-ounce) cartons egg substitute
1 (8-ounce) carton low-fat sour cream
8 cups hot cooked egg noodles (about 12 ounces uncooked)
Cooking spray
⅓ cup coarsely crushed cornflakes

1. Preheat oven to 350°.

2. Combine first 9 ingredients in a large bowl, and stir well. Add noodles, and toss gently to coat. Spoon mixture into a 13- x 9-inch baking dish coated with cooking spray. Sprinkle cornflakes over noodle mixture; cover and bake at 350° for 30 minutes. Uncover and bake an additional 10 minutes. Yield: 12 servings.

POINTS: 5; Exchanges: 3 Starch, ½ Lean Meat
Per serving: CAL 270 (13% from fat); PRO 13.3g; FAT 4g (sat 1.8g); CARB 42.9g; FIB 2.1g; CHOL 8mg; IRON 1.9mg; SOD 312mg; CALC 64mg

Cream Cheese Brûlée With Raspberries

1 (12-ounce) can evaporated skim milk
⅓ cup firmly packed light brown sugar
2 tablespoons cornstarch
3 large egg whites, lightly beaten
1 large egg, lightly beaten
1 (8-ounce) tub light cream cheese
1 teaspoon vanilla extract
1½ cups fresh raspberries
8 teaspoons light brown sugar

1. Combine first 5 ingredients in the top of a double boiler; stir well. Cook over simmering water 4 minutes or until thick, stirring constantly with a whisk. Remove from heat; add cream cheese and vanilla, stirring until smooth. Gently fold in raspberries.

2. Spoon ½ cup mixture into each of 8 (6-ounce) ramekins or custard cups. Let cool. Cover and chill at least 4 hours.

3. Sprinkle each serving with 1 teaspoon brown sugar. Place ramekins on a baking sheet; broil 1 minute or until sugar melts. Serve immediately. Yield: 8 servings.

POINTS: 4; Exchanges: 1 Starch, 1 Fat, ½ Sk Milk
Per serving: CAL 177 (28% from fat); PRO 8.4g; FAT 5.6g (sat 3.1g); CARB 23.4g; FIB 1.7g; CHOL 46mg; IRON 0.6mg; SOD 242mg; CALC 181mg

Citrus Sponge Pudding

As it bakes, this dessert forms two layers: a creamy pudding nestled beneath a spongy cake top.

1 cup 1% low-fat milk
½ cup pineapple juice
1 teaspoon grated orange rind
1 teaspoon grated lemon rind
⅓ cup fresh lemon juice
2 tablespoons stick margarine, melted
3 large egg yolks
¾ cup granulated sugar
⅓ cup all-purpose flour
¼ teaspoon salt
3 large egg whites (at room temperature)
Cooking spray
1 teaspoon powdered sugar

1. Preheat oven to 350°.

2. Combine first 7 ingredients in a medium bowl; stir well with a whisk. Set aside. Combine granulated sugar, flour, and salt in a large bowl. Gradually add milk mixture, stirring well (batter will be thin).

3. Beat egg whites with clean, dry beaters at high speed of a mixer until stiff peaks form. Gently stir one-fourth of egg whites into batter; gently fold in remaining egg whites.

4. Pour batter into a 1½-quart casserole dish coated with cooking spray. Place casserole dish in an 8-inch square baking dish, and add hot water to baking dish to a depth of 1 inch. Bake at 350° for 50 minutes or until golden brown.

The texture of Creamy Buttercup Pudding comes from the squash, which is reminiscent of sweet potato.

Sprinkle evenly with powdered sugar. Serve pudding warm or chilled. Yield: 6 servings.

POINTS: 5; Exchanges: 2½ Starch, 1 Fat
Per serving: CAL 227 (28% from fat); PRO 5.3g; FAT 7g (sat 1.8g); CARB 36.7g; FIB 0.2g; CHOL 111mg; IRON 0.7mg; SOD 194mg; CALC 71mg

Creamy Buttercup Pudding

1 (1½-pound) buttercup squash
1½ cups skim milk
¼ cup firmly packed brown sugar
1 tablespoon cornstarch
¼ teaspoon ground cinnamon
⅛ teaspoon ground nutmeg
⅛ teaspoon ground allspice
1 large egg
5 teaspoons gingersnap crumbs

1. Pierce squash several times with a fork; place in an 11- x 7-inch baking dish. Microwave at HIGH 4 to 5 minutes, rotating dish a half-turn after 2 minutes. Cut squash in half lengthwise; discard seeds and membrane. Place squash halves, cut sides down, in baking dish. Cover with heavy-duty plastic wrap, and microwave at HIGH 4 to 6 minutes or until very tender, rotating dish a half-turn every 2 minutes. Let cool slightly. Remove 1 cup squash pulp; reserve remaining squash pulp for another use.
2. Place 1 cup squash pulp, milk, and next 5

ingredients in a food processor; process until smooth. Add egg; process until well blended. Pour into a large bowl; microwave at HIGH 7½ to 10 minutes or until thick, stirring every 1½ minutes with a whisk. Spoon squash mixture evenly into 5 dessert dishes; cover and chill. Sprinkle 1 teaspoon cookie crumbs over each pudding. Yield: 5 servings.

POINTS: 2; Exchanges: 1 Starch
Per serving: CAL 99 (14% from fat); PRO 4.2g; FAT 1.5g (sat 0.5g); CARB 17.7g; FIB 0.5g; CHOL 46mg; IRON 0.7mg; SOD 58mg; CALC 123mg

Double-Chocolate Satin Pudding
The flavor of this rich pudding will remind you of dark-chocolate candy bars.

⅓ cup sugar
2 tablespoons cornstarch
2 tablespoons unsweetened cocoa
1 teaspoon instant espresso or 2 teaspoons instant coffee granules
⅛ teaspoon salt
1¾ cups 2% reduced-fat milk
1 (1-ounce) square semisweet chocolate, chopped
1 teaspoon vanilla extract

1. Combine first 5 ingredients in a saucepan; stir well. Gradually add milk, stirring with a whisk. Bring to a boil over medium heat, stirring constantly. Add chocolate; cook 1 minute, stirring constantly. Remove from heat; stir in vanilla. Pour into a bowl; cover surface of pudding with plastic wrap, and chill 2 hours. Yield: 4 servings (serving size: ½ cup).

POINTS: 4; Exchanges: 1½ Starch, ½ L-F Milk
Per serving: CAL 182 (23% from fat); PRO 4.8g; FAT 4.6g (sat 3g); CARB 31.2g; FIB 0.2g; CHOL 8mg; IRON 0.8mg; SOD 126mg; CALC 138mg

Cherry Clafouti
To enjoy the full flavor and just-right texture of the national dessert of France, serve it before it cools.

1 (16-ounce) can pitted dark sweet cherries in heavy syrup, drained
Cooking spray
2⅔ cups 2% reduced-fat milk
¾ cup all-purpose flour

½ cup granulated sugar
2 teaspoons vanilla extract
¼ teaspoon salt
1 large egg
1 large egg white
¼ cup granulated sugar
1 tablespoon powdered sugar
2⅔ cups vanilla low-fat frozen yogurt

1. Preheat oven to 375°.

2. Place cherries in an 8-inch square baking dish or deep-dish quiche dish coated with cooking spray; set aside.

3. Combine milk and next 6 ingredients; stir well with a whisk. Pour mixture over cherries, and sprinkle with ¼ cup granulated sugar. Bake at 375° for 1 hour and 55 minutes or until set. Sift powdered sugar over surface of pudding. Serve warm, and top each serving with ⅓ cup frozen yogurt. Yield: 8 servings.

POINTS: 5; **Exchanges:** 2½ Starch, ½ L-F Milk
Per serving: CAL 234 (12% from fat); PRO 6.2g; FAT 3g (sat 1.6g); CARB 46.1g; FIB 0.4g; CHOL 36mg; IRON 0.8mg; SOD 141mg; CALC 139mg

Queen of Puddings

5 (1-ounce) slices white bread
½ cup sugar, divided
3 tablespoons stick margarine, melted
1½ teaspoons grated lemon rind
3 cups skim milk
2 large eggs, separated (at room temperature)
1 teaspoon vanilla extract
Cooking spray
¾ cup seedless raspberry jam, melted

1. Preheat oven to 400°.

2. Trim crust from bread slices; cut bread into ¾-inch cubes, and place in a large bowl. Combine 2 tablespoons sugar, margarine, and lemon rind; stir well. Drizzle sugar mixture over bread cubes, tossing well. Arrange bread cubes in a single layer on a baking sheet. Bake at 400° for 10 minutes or until crisp. Reduce oven temperature to 350°.

3. Combine 3 tablespoons sugar, milk, egg yolks, and vanilla in a saucepan; stir well with a whisk.

Place over medium heat, and cook 5 minutes or until warm, stirring constantly (mixture should only be warm and not thicken).

4. Place ⅓ cup bread cubes into each of 6 (6-ounce) ramekins or custard cups coated with cooking spray. Pour about ½ cup milk mixture into each cup. Place cups in a 13- x 9-inch baking pan. Pour hot water into pan to depth of 1 inch. Bake at 350° for 1 hour or until a knife inserted near center comes out clean. Remove from oven (leave cups in water bath).

5. Drizzle raspberry jam evenly over top of each pudding; set aside.

6. Beat egg whites with clean, dry beaters at high speed of a mixer until foamy. Gradually add remaining 3 tablespoons sugar, 1 tablespoon at a time, beating until soft peaks form. Spread meringue evenly over each pudding, sealing to edge of cups. Bake at 350° for 10 minutes or until meringue is lightly browned. Remove cups from water. Serve warm. Yield: 6 servings.

POINTS: 7; **Exchanges:** 3½ Starch, 1 Fat
Per serving: CAL 333 (23% from fat); PRO 8.5g; FAT 8.6g (sat 2g); CARB 54.4g; FIB 0.5g; CHOL 76mg; IRON 1.0mg; SOD 279mg; CALC 188mg

The keys to a successful Cherry Clafouti (pronounced cla-foo-TEE) are minimal use of flour and a hot oven in which to cook it quickly.

Ice Caps

THERE'S NO BETTER WAY TO END THE DAY
THAN WITH ONE OF THESE COOL TREATS.

*T*here's something about a cooler temperature that snaps the taste buds

to attention and makes a dessert more satisfying. If you've ever taken a

candy bar and put it in the freezer, you know what we mean. And while

frozen desserts are heavenly in the heat of summer, they're a pleasure worth

savoring year-round. So to appease a sweet tooth with an icy preference,

reach for one of these frosty, convenient treats. There's everything from

Lemon Ice makes Caramel Ice Cream for the traditionalist to Baked Alaska for the daring. And
a simple and
refreshing palate many of the recipes in this chapter can be prepared ahead of time so you can
cleanser or light
dessert. simply pull them out whenever guests—or urges—arrive.

Baked Alaska

Lemon Ice

3 cups boiling water
1 cup sugar
2 teaspoons grated lemon rind
½ cup fresh lemon juice
Mint leaves (optional)
Sugared lemon zest (optional)

1. Combine boiling water and sugar in a medium bowl; stir until sugar dissolves. Let cool. Stir in lemon rind and juice. Pour mixture into a 9-inch nonaluminum square baking pan or dish. Cover and freeze until firm. Let stand at room temperature 10 minutes before serving. Garnish with mint leaves and sugared lemon zest, if desired. Yield: 4 servings (serving size: ½ cup).

Note: To make sugared lemon zest, dip long strips of lemon rind in water, and roll in sugar.

POINTS: 4; **Exchanges:** 3½ Starch
Per serving: CAL 201 (0% from fat); PRO 0.1g; FAT 0g (sat 0g); CARB 52.7g; FIB 0.1g; CHOL 0mg; IRON 0mg; SOD 1mg; CALC 4mg

Baked Alaska

4 cups raspberry-vanilla swirl frozen yogurt, slightly softened
½ cup sifted cake flour
½ teaspoon baking powder
⅛ teaspoon salt
2 large egg yolks
½ cup sugar
2 tablespoons water
1 teaspoon vanilla extract
3 large egg whites (at room temperature)
¼ cup sugar
Cooking spray
3 tablespoons seedless raspberry jam
4 large egg whites (at room temperature)
½ teaspoon cream of tartar
⅓ cup sugar
3 tablespoons water
Fresh raspberries (optional)
Mint leaves (optional)

1. Spoon yogurt into a 7- or 8-inch-diameter deep bowl lined with heavy-duty plastic wrap, pressing yogurt with the back of a spoon to pack tightly. Cover and freeze until firm.

2. Preheat oven to 350°.

3. Combine flour, baking powder, and salt in a bowl; stir well, and set aside. Beat egg yolks in a large bowl at high speed of a mixer for 2 minutes. Gradually add ½ cup sugar, beating until thick and pale (about 2 minutes). Add 2 tablespoons water and vanilla, beating at low speed until blended. Add flour mixture; beat well.

4. Beat 3 egg whites with clean, dry beaters at high speed of a mixer until foamy. Gradually add ¼ cup sugar, 1 tablespoon at a time, beating until stiff peaks form. Gently stir one-fourth of egg white mixture into batter; gently fold in remaining egg white mixture.

5. Pour batter into an 8-inch square baking pan coated with cooking spray. Bake at 350° for 20 minutes or until cake springs back when touched lightly in center. Let cool 5 minutes in pan on a wire rack. Loosen cake from sides of pan, using a narrow metal spatula, and turn out onto wire rack; let cool completely. Increase oven temperature to 500°.

6. Place cake, bottom side up, on an ovenproof platter. Spread raspberry jam over cake. Remove frozen yogurt from freezer; let stand at room temperature 5 minutes. Invert yogurt onto top of cake; remove bowl and plastic wrap. Cover and freeze at least 15 minutes. (You can assemble the recipe to this point one day ahead and store, covered, in the freezer.)

7. Beat 4 egg whites and cream of tartar with clean, dry beaters at high speed of a mixer until stiff peaks form; set aside. Combine ⅓ cup sugar and 3 tablespoons water in a saucepan; bring to a boil; cook, without stirring, until candy thermometer registers 238°. Pour mixture in a thin stream over egg whites, beating at high speed. Spread meringue over yogurt and around sides of cake (yogurt and cake should be completely covered with meringue). Bake at 500° for 2 minutes or until meringue is golden (do not overcook or frozen yogurt will melt). Serve immediately. Garnish with fresh raspberries and mint leaves, if desired. Yield: 9 servings (serving size: 1 slice).

One of many theories about the origin of Baked Alaska claims that it was created to commemorate the United States' purchase of Alaska.

Note: You can substitute any flavor frozen yogurt and a complementary flavored jam, if desired.

POINTS: 6; **Exchanges:** 4 Starch
Per serving: CAL 291 (8% from fat); PRO 8.7g; FAT 2.5g (sat 0.4g); CARB 60.2g; FIB 0.1g; CHOL 54mg; IRON 0.7mg; SOD118mg; CALC 195mg

Apricot-Yogurt Tortoni

You must move quickly to assemble and freeze this dessert.

1   (12-ounce) package reduced-fat vanilla wafers, crushed
1   (½-gallon) vanilla fat-free frozen yogurt, softened and divided
1   teaspoon almond extract
Cooking spray
1   (18-ounce) jar apricot preserves
1   (17-ounce) can apricot halves in light syrup, undrained
1   (2.25-ounce) package sliced almonds, toasted

1. Combine vanilla wafer crumbs, 1¼ cups frozen yogurt, and almond extract; stir well. Divide mixture in half.

2. Coat a 13- x 9-inch baking dish with cooking spray; spread half of wafer mixture over bottom of dish. Spread remaining frozen yogurt over wafer mixture in dish. Spread apricot preserves over frozen yogurt, and top with remaining wafer mixture. Cover and freeze at least 8 hours. Cut into squares; top evenly with apricots and a small amount of syrup. Sprinkle with almonds. Yield: 15 servings.

POINTS: 6; **Exchanges:** 3½ Starch
Per serving: CAL 278 (17% from fat); PRO 6.5g; FAT 5.3g (sat 0.2g); CARB 51.5g; FIB 0.9g; CHOL 0mg; IRON 0.9mg; SOD 88mg; CALC 136mg

Ginger-Mango Gelato

2   cups peeled diced mango
2   tablespoons fresh lime juice
2   teaspoons minced crystallized ginger
1½ cups water
¾   cup sugar
Mint sprigs (optional)

1. Place diced mango, lime juice, and crystallized ginger in a blender or food processor, and process

until mixture is smooth. Set aside. Combine water and sugar in a small saucepan; bring to a boil, and cook 1 minute, stirring constantly. Remove from heat, and stir in mango mixture. Let cool to room temperature.

2. Pour the mixture into the freezer can of an ice cream freezer, and freeze according to the manufacturer's instructions. Garnish with mint sprigs, if desired. Yield: 6 servings (serving size: ½ cup).

POINTS: 3; **Exchanges:** 1½ Starch, ½ Fruit
Per serving: CAL 136 (1% from fat); PRO 0.3g; FAT 0.2g (sat 0g); CARB 35.3g; FIB 0.8g; CHOL 0mg; IRON 0.2mg; SOD 2mg; CALC 8mg

Kona Coffee Ice Cream in Chocolate Cookie Cups

If you do not have a fine sieve, use a coffee filter-lined sieve to strain the coffee mixture.

6   cups 2% reduced-fat milk
¾   cup evaporated skim milk
⅔   cup ground Kona coffee
¾   cup sugar
⅔   cup light-colored corn syrup
Chocolate Cookie Cups
Grated semisweet chocolate (optional)

1. Combine reduced-fat milk, evaporated milk, and Kona coffee in a saucepan. Place over low heat, and cook 30 minutes. Remove from heat; cover and let stand 20 minutes. Pour coffee mixture through a fine sieve into a medium bowl, and discard coffee grounds. Add sugar and corn syrup, and stir well. Pour mixture into the freezer can of an ice cream freezer, and freeze according to the manufacturer's instructions. Spoon ice cream into a freezer-safe container; cover and freeze 2 hours or until firm. Serve ice cream in Chocolate Cookie Cups. Sprinkle evenly with grated semisweet chocolate, if desired. Yield: 12 servings (serving size: ⅔ cup ice cream and 1 cookie cup).

POINTS: 5; **Exchanges:** 2½ Starch, ½ L-F Milk
Per serving: CAL 249 (18% from fat); PRO 6.8g; FAT 5.1g (sat 1.9g); CARB 44.6g; FIB 0.3g; CHOL 10mg; IRON 0.4mg; SOD 184mg; CALC 198mg

Chocolate Cookie Cups:

½   cup sugar
3   tablespoons all-purpose flour
3   tablespoons quick-cooking oats
2   tablespoons finely chopped almonds
1   tablespoon unsweetened cocoa
¼   teaspoon salt
2   tablespoons stick margarine, melted
½   teaspoon vanilla extract
¼   teaspoon almond extract
3   large egg whites, lightly beaten
Cooking spray

1. Preheat oven to 350°.

2. Combine first 6 ingredients in a medium bowl. Combine margarine, extracts, and egg whites; stir well. Add to sugar mixture, stirring just until moist.

3. Coat baking sheets with cooking spray; using a finger, trace 12 (3-inch) circles in cooking spray on baking sheets. Spoon 1 tablespoon batter into center of each circle; spread batter to outside edge of each circle. Bake at 350° for 10 minutes or until edges appear dry.

4. Remove cookies from pan immediately, and place each cookie over an inverted 6-ounce custard cup (or jar) coated with cooking spray. Shape cookies around custard cups to form cookie cups; let cool completely. Yield: 1 dozen.

Frozen Strawberry Dessert

1   (3-ounce) package strawberry gelatin
1   cup boiling water
1   quart vanilla low-fat frozen yogurt, softened
1   (8-ounce) can unsweetened crushed pineapple, undrained

1. Combine strawberry gelatin and 1 cup boiling water; stir 2 minutes or until gelatin dissolves. Add frozen yogurt and crushed pineapple,

Hawaiian coffee imparts a rich, robust flavor to Kona Coffee Ice Cream in Chocolate Cookie Cups.

Experience a taste of the South with Bourbon-Raisin Ice Cream and Benne Seed Wafers (page 45).

stirring until yogurt melts. Pour into a 9-inch square baking pan. Cover and freeze 8 hours or until firm. Let stand at room temperature at least 10 minutes before serving. Cut into squares. Yield: 12 servings.

POINTS: 2; **Exchanges:** 1½ Starch
Per serving: CAL 112 (8% from fat); PRO 2.6g; FAT 1.0g (sat 0.7g); CARB 23.2g; FIB 0.1g; CHOL 6mg; IRON 0.1mg; SOD 74mg; CALC 69mg

Bourbon-Raisin Ice Cream

2   cups skim milk
1   cup sugar
½   cup milk chocolate-covered raisins, chopped
½   cup egg substitute
¼   cup bourbon
½   teaspoon vanilla extract
1   (12-ounce) can evaporated skim milk
Mint leaves (optional)

1. Combine first 7 ingredients in a large bowl; stir well. Pour mixture into the freezer can of an ice cream freezer, and freeze according to manufacturer's instructions. Spoon ice cream into a freezer-safe container; cover and freeze 2 hours or until firm. Garnish with mint leaves, if desired. Yield: 8 servings (serving size: 1 cup).

POINTS: 5; **Exchanges:** 2½ Starch, ½ Sk Milk
Per serving: CAL 225 (8% from fat); PRO 7.0g; FAT 1.9g (sat 1.2g); CARB 40.9g; FIB 0.6g; CHOL 3mg; IRON 0.5mg; SOD 108mg; CALC 214mg

Daiquiri Ice With Kiwifruit

2¼ cups water
¾   cup sugar
½   cup white rum
1   tablespoon grated lime rind
½   cup fresh lime juice
3   kiwifruit, peeled and thinly sliced
Mint sprigs (optional)
Lime slices (optional)

1. Combine water and sugar in a saucepan; stir well. Place over low heat; cook 2 minutes or until sugar dissolves. Remove from heat; stir in rum, lime rind, and juice. Pour mixture into the freezer can of an ice cream freezer, and freeze according to manufacturer's instructions.

2. Arrange kiwifruit slices and small scoops of daiquiri ice on individual dessert plates, and garnish with mint sprigs and lime slices, if desired. Yield: 6 servings (serving size: ½ cup ice and ½ kiwifruit).

POINTS: 3; **Exchanges:** 2 Starch
Per serving: CAL 168 (2% from fat); PRO 0.6g; FAT 0.3g (sat 0g); CARB 31.4g; FIB 1.3g; CHOL 0mg; IRON 0.2mg; SOD 1mg; CALC 13mg

Strawberry-Champagne Sorbet

This lightly sweetened sorbet pairs fresh strawberries and champagne—a divine dessert duo.

½   cup sugar
½   cup water
1   (10-ounce) package frozen strawberries in syrup, thawed and undrained
1½ cups dry champagne
2   tablespoons lemon juice
½   cup sliced fresh strawberries

1. Combine sugar and water in a heavy saucepan; cook over medium heat until sugar dissolves, stirring constantly. Remove sugar syrup from heat; let cool.

2. Place thawed strawberries in a blender or food processor; process until smooth. Pour puréed strawberries through a sieve into an 8-inch square baking pan, pressing strawberries with the back of a spoon to extract juice. Discard pulp and seeds. Stir sugar syrup, champagne, and lemon juice into strawberry purée. Cover and freeze at least 4 hours.

3. Break frozen mixture into chunks. Place half of frozen chunks in food processor, and process until smooth. Return to pan; place pan in freezer. Repeat procedure with remaining frozen chunks. Cover and freeze until firm.

4. Spoon sorbet into 6 individual stemmed glasses, and top evenly with sliced fresh strawberries. Yield: 6 servings (serving size: ½ cup sorbet and about 1 tablespoon sliced strawberries).

POINTS: 2; **Exchanges:** 1 Fruit, ½ Starch
Per serving: CAL 129 (1% from fat); PRO 0.6g; FAT 0.2g (sat 0g); CARB 22.1g; FIB 1.6g; CHOL 0mg; IRON 0.6mg; SOD 3mg; CALC 9mg

Frozen Raspberry Brownie Bars

1   (20.5-ounce) package light fudge brownie
    mix
Cooking spray
4   cups raspberry low-fat frozen yogurt,
    softened
½   cup chocolate graham snack crumbs
2   cups fresh raspberries

1. Preheat oven to 350°.

2. Prepare brownie mix according to package directions, using a 13- x 9-inch baking pan coated with cooking spray. Bake at 350° for 20 minutes. Let cool completely.

3. Spread frozen yogurt evenly over cooled brownies. Sprinkle crumbs over yogurt; cover and freeze 5 hours or until yogurt is firm. Cut into bars, and top each bar with fresh raspberries. Yield: 16 servings (serving size: 1 bar and 2 tablespoons raspberries).

POINTS: 4; **Exchanges:** 3 Starch
Per serving: CAL 221 (13% from fat); PRO 3.3g; FAT 3.1g (sat 1.6g); CARB 44.3g; FIB 1.1g; CHOL 5mg; IRON 0.5mg; SOD 174mg; CALC 51mg

Frozen Chocolate Roulage

Cooking spray
1   tablespoon sifted cake flour
¾   cup sifted cake flour
⅓   cup unsweetened cocoa
⅓   cup sugar
1   teaspoon baking powder
½   teaspoon baking soda
¼   teaspoon salt
½   cup water
⅓   cup vegetable oil
2   teaspoons vanilla extract
5   large egg whites (at room temperature)
⅓   cup sugar
¼   cup sifted cake flour
2   tablespoons unsweetened cocoa, divided
2   cups raspberry low-fat frozen yogurt,
    softened

1. Preheat oven to 325°.

2. Coat a 15- x 10-inch jelly-roll pan with cooking spray; line with wax paper. Coat wax paper with cooking spray, and dust with 1 tablespoon flour; remove excess flour. Set aside.

3. Combine ¾ cup flour and next 5 ingredients in a large bowl; stir well. Add water, oil, and vanilla; stir until smooth. Set aside.

With Frozen Raspberry Brownie Bars in the freezer, you always have dessert on hand.

Maple-Rum Banana Sundae

4. Beat egg whites with clean, dry beaters at high speed of a mixer until foamy. Gradually add ⅓ cup sugar, 1 tablespoon at a time, beating until stiff peaks form. Fold egg whites into batter. Sift ¼ cup flour over batter, and fold until blended.

5. Pour batter into prepared pan, spreading evenly. Bake at 325° for 12 minutes or until cake pulls away from sides of pan. Let cool in pan on a wire rack 10 minutes. Invert cake onto a dish-towel dusted with 1 tablespoon cocoa; peel off wax paper. Starting at long side, roll up cake and towel together; let cool, seam side down, on a wire rack.

6. Unroll cake, and sprinkle with remaining 1 tablespoon cocoa. Spread frozen yogurt over cake, leaving a ½-inch margin. Reroll cake, and place on heavy-duty plastic wrap, seam side down. Wrap tightly in plastic wrap, and freeze until firm. Yield: 14 servings.

POINTS: 4; **Exchanges:** 1½ Starch, 1 Fat
Per serving: CAL 164 (34% from fat); PRO 3.2g; FAT 6.2g (sat 1.2g); CARB 23.8g; FIB 0g; CHOL 3mg; IRON 0.6mg; SOD 110mg; CALC 32mg

Coffee-Toffee Dessert

1 (10¾-ounce) loaf angel food cake
1 tablespoon instant coffee granules
1 tablespoon hot water
1 teaspoon vanilla extract
4 cups vanilla fat-free frozen yogurt, softened
4 (1.4-ounce) chocolate-covered toffee candy bars, crushed
2 tablespoons Kahlúa (coffee-flavored liqueur)
1 (8-ounce) tub frozen reduced-calorie whipped topping, thawed

1. Cut cake into ½-inch-thick slices. Arrange cake slices, overlapping, in bottom of a 9-inch springform pan; set aside.

2. Combine instant coffee granules, hot water, and vanilla in a medium bowl; stir well. Add frozen yogurt and crushed candy bars, and stir well. Spread yogurt mixture over cake slices. Gently stir Kahlúa into whipped topping, and

spread over yogurt mixture. Cover and freeze 8 hours or until firm. Yield: 14 servings (serving size: 1 wedge).

POINTS: 5; **Exchanges:** 2½ Starch, ½ Fat
Per serving: CAL 228 (24% from fat); PRO 4.1g; FAT 6.1g (sat 3.9g); CARB 35g; FIB 0g; CHOL 0mg; IRON 0.2mg; SOD 111mg; CALC 109mg

Maple-Rum Banana Sundaes

2 large ripe bananas
½ cup maple syrup
6 tablespoons dark rum
1 teaspoon stick margarine
1⅓ cups vanilla fat-free ice cream
4 teaspoons chopped pecans, toasted

1. Peel bananas, and cut in half lengthwise. Cut each half into 4 equal portions; set aside.

2. Combine maple syrup, rum, and margarine in a large skillet. Place over medium-low heat, and cook until margarine melts. Add banana pieces; cook 1 minute. Turn banana pieces over, and cook an additional 1 minute.

3. Arrange 4 banana pieces on each of 4 dessert plates; top each with ⅓ cup ice cream, ½ tablespoon sauce, and 1 teaspoon pecans. Yield: 4 servings.

POINTS: 5; **Exchanges:** 2½ Starch, 1 Fruit
Per serving: CAL 256 (14% from fat); PRO 2.8g; FAT 4g (sat 1.1g); CARB 54.7g; FIB 1.6g; CHOL 6mg; IRON 0.7mg; SOD 62mg; CALC 98mg

Frozen Chocolate-Cherry Squares

6 chocolate wafer cookies, crushed
2 teaspoons stick margarine, melted
Cooking spray
6 cups chocolate low-fat ice cream, softened
1 cup pitted diced fresh sweet cherries
2 tablespoons white rum
3 tablespoons semisweet chocolate chips
1 teaspoon skim milk

1. Combine wafer crumbs and margarine; stir well. Sprinkle half of crumb mixture on bottom of an 8-inch square baking pan coated with cooking spray. Set aside.

¼ teaspoon vanilla extract
1¼ cups coffee low-fat frozen yogurt, softened
20 chocolate wafer cookies

1. Combine sugar, corn syrup, cocoa, and milk in a small heavy saucepan; bring mixture to a boil over medium-low heat, stirring frequently with a whisk. Cook 2 minutes or until thick, stirring frequently. Remove from heat; stir in margarine and vanilla. Pour mixture into a bowl; cover and chill thoroughly.

2. Spread 2 tablespoons frozen yogurt onto each of 10 cookies; top with about 1 teaspoon syrup mixture and remaining cookies, pressing gently. Freeze at least 1 hour. Yield: 10 sandwiches (serving size: 1 sandwich).

POINTS: 2; **Exchanges:** 1 Starch, ½ Fat
Per serving: CAL 103 (30% from fat); PRO 1.7g; FAT 3.4g (sat 1.1g); CARB 16.7g; FIB 0g; CHOL 11mg; IRON 0.4mg; SOD 62mg; CALC 38mg

Praline-Chocolate Bombe

If you prefer not to use praline liqueur, drizzle each wedge with 2 teaspoons fat-free caramel-flavored sundae syrup.

1 cup reduced-fat gingersnap cookie crumbs (about 25 cookies)
2 tablespoons reduced-calorie stick margarine, melted
4 cups praline-and-caramel low-fat ice cream, softened
2 individually wrapped commercial low-fat brownies (such as Snack Wells), cut into cubes
¼ cup finely chopped pecans, toasted
¼ cup fat-free caramel-flavored sundae syrup
½ cup plus 2 tablespoons praline liqueur

1. Line a 1½-quart bowl with heavy-duty plastic wrap. Combine cookie crumbs and margarine; stir well. Press crumb mixture into bottom and up sides of bowl, leaving a 1-inch margin around top of bowl. Combine ice cream and next 3 ingredients; stir well. Spoon ice cream mixture into bowl. Cover and freeze at least 8 hours.

2. Remove ice cream mixture from freezer; let stand at room temperature 5 minutes. Invert

These Frozen Mud Pie Sandwiches will make you forget the store-bought ones you grew up with.

2. Combine ice cream, cherries, and rum in a bowl; stir well. Spread ice cream mixture into prepared pan.

3. Combine chocolate chips and milk in a small saucepan. Place over low heat, and cook just until chocolate melts. Drizzle chocolate mixture over ice cream mixture. Sprinkle with remaining half of crumb mixture. Cover and freeze until firm. Cut into squares. Yield: 9 servings.

POINTS: 4; **Exchanges:** 2 Starch, ½ Sk Milk
Per serving: CAL 205 (20% from fat); PRO 5.8g; FAT 4.6g (sat 0.8g); CARB 34.6g; FIB 0.4g; CHOL 0mg; IRON 0.2mg; SOD 88mg; CALC 139mg

Frozen Mud Pie Sandwiches

This summertime ice cream sandwich has its own fudge sauce. These sandwiches can be stored in the freezer for up to four days.

2 tablespoons sugar
2 tablespoons light-colored corn syrup
1½ tablespoons unsweetened cocoa
1 tablespoon 1% low-fat milk
1 teaspoon stick margarine

onto a serving platter; remove bowl and plastic wrap. Cut into wedges. Drizzle 1 tablespoon liqueur over each wedge. Yield: 10 servings.

POINTS: 6; **Exchanges:** 3 Starch, 1 Fat
Per serving: CAL 266 (25% from fat); PRO 3.5g; FAT 7.4g (sat 2g); CARB 45.8g; FIB 1.3g; CHOL 8mg; IRON 0.9mg; SOD 127mg; CALC 85mg

Frozen Strawberry Margarita Squares

6   cups vanilla fat-free ice cream, softened
2   cups frozen unsweetened whole strawberries, halved
¼   cup fresh lime juice
2   tablespoons tequila
2   tablespoons triple sec (orange-flavored liqueur)
Cooking spray
20 unsalted pretzel sticks, crushed

1. Combine first 5 ingredients in a bowl; stir well. Spread into an 8-inch square baking pan coated with cooking spray; sprinkle with crushed pretzels. Cover and freeze until firm. Cut into squares. Yield: 9 servings.

POINTS: 3; **Exchanges:** 1½ Starch, ½ Sk Milk
Per serving: CAL 166 (0% from fat); PRO 6.2g; FAT 0.1g (sat 0g); CARB 32.8g; FIB 0.3g; CHOL 0mg; IRON 0.3mg; SOD 104mg; CALC 166mg

Vanilla-Buttermilk Ice Cream

1   (6-inch) vanilla bean, split lengthwise
2   cups 2% reduced-fat milk
¾   cup sugar
1   cup low-fat buttermilk
1   (12-ounce) can evaporated skim milk

1. Scrape seeds from vanilla bean; place seeds and bean in a saucepan. Add 2% reduced-fat milk to pan; cook over medium-low heat to 180° or until tiny bubbles form around edge of pan (do not boil). Remove from heat; discard vanilla bean.
2. Pour vanilla-milk mixture into a large bowl; add sugar, stirring until sugar dissolves. Stir in buttermilk and evaporated milk. Cover and chill.
3. Pour chilled mixture into the freezer can of an ice cream freezer, and freeze according to manufacturer's instructions. Spoon ice cream into a freezer-safe container; cover and freeze at least 1 hour or until firm. Yield: 8 servings (serving size: 1 cup).

POINTS: 3; **Exchanges:** 1 Sk Milk, 1 Starch
Per serving: CAL 151 (11% from fat); PRO 6.4g; FAT 1.7g (sat 0.8g); CARB 28g; FIB 0g; CHOL 7mg; IRON 0.2mg; SOD 95mg; CALC 235mg

Caramel Ice Cream Dessert

A gooey caramel topping and a hearty mix of oats, brown sugar, and pecans cloak a frosty layer of ice cream in this easy make-ahead dessert.

1   cup all-purpose flour
½   cup quick-cooking oats
⅓   cup firmly packed brown sugar
¼   cup finely chopped pecans
¼   cup reduced-calorie stick margarine, melted
Cooking spray
1   (12.25-ounce) jar fat-free caramel ice cream topping
4   cups vanilla fat-free ice cream, softened

1. Preheat oven to 350°.
2. Combine flour, quick-cooking oats, brown sugar, and pecans in a medium bowl; stir well.

If you think vanilla is plain or dull, you haven't tasted Vanilla-Buttermilk Ice Cream and Vanilla Wafers (page 48).

1. Combine all ingredients in a pitcher; stir until sugar dissolves. Pour into ice cube trays; freeze 4 hours or until firm.

2. Let stand at room temperature 10 minutes. Place frozen cubes in a food processor; process until smooth. Spoon into chilled dishes or glasses. Garnish with mint leaves, if desired. Serve immediately. Yield: 8 servings (serving size: 1 cup).

Note: If you do not have ice cube trays, you can freeze coffee mixture in a baking pan. Break frozen mixture into chunks, and place chunks in food processor.

POINTS: 2; **Exchanges:** 1 Starch
Per serving: CAL 89 (10% from fat); PRO 3.1g; FAT 1g (sat 0.6g); CARB 17.g; FIB 0g; CHOL 4mg; IRON 0.4mg; SOD 48mg; CALC 114mg

Frozen Yogurt With Rum-Raisin Sauce

⅓ cup firmly packed brown sugar
2 tablespoons water
1 tablespoon stick margarine
1½ tablespoons all-purpose flour
1¼ cups 2% reduced-fat milk
⅓ cup raisins
½ teaspoon rum flavoring
3 cups vanilla low-fat frozen yogurt

1. Combine first 3 ingredients in a small saucepan; stir well. Place over medium heat, and cook 3 minutes or until margarine melts, stirring occasionally. Place flour in a small bowl; gradually add milk, stirring with a whisk until blended. Add milk mixture and raisins to pan; stir well. Cook 5 minutes or until thick, stirring constantly. Remove from heat; stir in rum flavoring. Serve over frozen yogurt. Yield: 6 servings (serving size: ½ cup frozen yogurt and ¼ cup sauce).

Note: The sauce can be made in advance and reheated in the microwave. Place sauce in a 2-cup glass measure; microwave at HIGH 1 minute or until warm, stirring every 30 seconds.

POINTS: 5; **Exchanges:** 2 Starch, ½ L-F Milk
Per serving: CAL 216 (22% from fat); PRO 5g; FAT 4.8g (sat 2.4g); CARB 39.4g; FIB 0.5g; CHOL 14mg; IRON 0.5mg; SOD 87mg; CALC 173mg

Add margarine; stir until blended. Press mixture firmly into a 15- x 10-inch jelly-roll pan coated with cooking spray.

3. Bake at 350° for 12 minutes or until lightly browned. Let cool, and crumble.

4. Sprinkle two-thirds of crumbled oat mixture in bottom of a 9-inch springform pan coated with cooking spray. Drizzle with half of caramel topping. Spread ice cream over topping. Drizzle with remaining caramel topping; sprinkle with remaining crumbled oat mixture. Cover and freeze until firm. Yield: 12 servings (serving size: 1 slice).

POINTS: 5; **Exchanges:** 3 Starch
Per serving: CAL 252 (14% from fat); PRO 3.8g; FAT 4g (sat 0.2g); CARB 49.1g; FIB 0.7g; CHOL 0mg; IRON 1mg; SOD 145mg; CALC 91mg

Café au Lait Granita

3 cups hot strong brewed coffee
3 cups 1% low-fat milk
½ cup sugar
Mint leaves (optional)

Frozen Yogurt With
Rum-Raisin Sauce

Surprise Endings

EXPAND YOUR CULINARY HORIZONS WITH
THESE UNPREDICTABLE DESSERTS.

Pavlova is an Australian dessert named after the Russian ballerina Anna Pavlova.

There's something admirable about a woman who knows what she wants, but decisiveness isn't all it's cracked up to be. What indecisive women lack in certainty, they make up for in whimsy. Take desserts, for example. Among the decisive are the cake, custard, and frozen-dessert fans. The indecisive woman simply loves desserts so much she can't decide. So this chapter is devoted to her, the woman who craves baked fruit desserts one day and a light soufflé the next. And when she has a preference for dessert pancakes or tiramisu, we've got it covered. Even the decisive will waver once they discover recipes that don't fall into the classic categories of cakes or custards. So much for certainty.

Pavlova

Assemble and serve this dessert immediately so the meringue is still crunchy.

- 5 large egg whites (at room temperature)
- ¼ teaspoon salt
- 1 cup granulated sugar
- 4 teaspoons cornstarch
- ½ teaspoon vanilla extract
- ½ teaspoon white vinegar
- 4 cups assorted fresh berries
- 2 tablespoons powdered sugar
- 1½ cups vanilla low-fat ice cream, melted
- 1½ teaspoons Grand Marnier (orange-flavored liqueur) or ½ teaspoon extract of your choice

1. Preheat oven to 275°.

2. Cover a large baking sheet with parchment paper. Draw a 10-inch circle on parchment paper. Turn parchment paper over. Secure with masking tape; set aside.

3. Beat egg whites with clean, dry beaters at high speed of a mixer until foamy. Add salt, beating until stiff peaks form. Gradually add granulated sugar, 1 tablespoon at a time, beating until stiff peaks form (do not underbeat). Sprinkle cornstarch over egg white mixture; beat at low speed until well blended. Beat in vanilla and vinegar.

4. Spoon egg white mixture onto drawn circle. Using the back of a spoon, shape meringue into a "nest" with 2½-inch sides. Bake at 275° for 2 hours or until meringue is dry. Turn oven off; let meringue cool in closed oven at least 12 hours. Carefully remove meringue from paper; set aside.

5. Combine fresh berries and powdered sugar; toss well. Let stand 5 minutes. Combine melted low-fat ice cream and liqueur; stir well. Spoon berry mixture into center of meringue, and drizzle with melted ice cream mixture. Cut into wedges. Yield: 8 servings.

POINTS: 3; **Exchanges:** 2 Starch, ½ Fruit
Per serving: CAL 180 (7% from fat); PRO 3.5g; FAT 1.3g (sat 0.7g); CARB 39.4g; FIB 1.9g; CHOL 3mg; IRON 0.3mg; SOD 128mg; CALC 46mg

Cantaloupe and Blackberries With Almond Cream combines two of summer's most nutrient-packed fruits in a simple dessert.

Cantaloupe and Blackberries With Almond Cream

- ½ cup tub-style fat-free cream cheese, softened
- 2 tablespoons powdered sugar
- 1 tablespoon 1% low-fat milk
- ¼ teaspoon almond extract
- ½ (2½-pound) cantaloupe, peeled, seeded, and cut lengthwise into ¼-inch-thick slices
- 1 cup fresh blackberries
- 4 teaspoons sliced almonds, toasted
- Mint sprigs (optional)

1. Combine fat-free cream cheese, powdered sugar, low-fat milk, and almond extract in a bowl, and beat at high speed of a mixer until smooth. Arrange one-fourth of peeled cantaloupe slices, ¼ cup fresh blackberries, and 2 tablespoons cream cheese mixture on each of 4 dessert plates. Sprinkle each serving with 1 teaspoon toasted almonds. Garnish with mint sprigs, if desired. Yield: 4 servings.

POINTS: 1; **Exchanges:** 1 Fruit, 1 Very Lean Meat
Per serving: CAL 97 (13% from fat); PRO 5.4g; FAT 1.4g (sat 0.2g); CARB 15.9g; FIB 3.7g; CHOL 5mg; IRON 0.4mg; SOD 179mg; CALC 109mg

Razzle-Dazzle Berry Trifle

1½ cups boiling water
2 (3-ounce) packages raspberry-flavored gelatin
1 cup cold water
24 ice cubes
2 cups sliced banana
1 (21-ounce) can blueberry pie filling
4 cups (1-inch) cubed angel food cake
½ cup orange juice
1 (5.1-ounce) package vanilla instant pudding mix (not sugar-free)
2½ cups 2% reduced-fat milk
1 cup frozen reduced-calorie whipped topping, thawed
Fresh blueberries and fresh raspberries (optional)
Mint sprigs (optional)

1. Combine boiling water and gelatin in a bowl; stir until gelatin dissolves (about 2 minutes). Add cold water and ice cubes, stirring until slightly thick. Remove any unmelted ice cubes. Stir in banana and blueberry pie filling; set aside.

2. Place cake cubes in a trifle bowl. Drizzle orange juice over cake cubes; toss well. Spoon gelatin mixture over cake cubes; cover and chill 30 minutes.

3. Prepare pudding according to package directions, using 2½ cups of 2% reduced-fat milk. Fold whipped topping into pudding; spread over gelatin mixture. Cover and chill. Garnish with blueberries, raspberries, and mint, if desired. Yield: 11 servings (serving size: 1 cup).

POINTS: 6; **Exchanges:** 3½ Fruit, ½ Starch, ½ L-F Milk
Per serving: CAL 295 (6% from fat); PRO 5.1g; FAT 2g (sat 1.2g); CARB 65.4g; FIB 1.5g; CHOL 5mg; IRON 0.2mg; SOD 393mg; CALC 157mg

Orange Soufflé

Cooking spray
1 tablespoon granulated sugar
3 tablespoons all-purpose flour
¾ cup 2% reduced-fat milk
¼ cup granulated sugar
1 teaspoon grated orange rind
¼ cup fresh orange juice
5 large egg whites (at room temperature)
¼ teaspoon cream of tartar
Dash of salt
2 tablespoons granulated sugar
1 teaspoon powdered sugar

1. Preheat oven to 375°.

2. Coat a 1½-quart soufflé dish with cooking spray; sprinkle with 1 tablespoon sugar. Set aside.

3. Place flour in a saucepan. Gradually add milk, stirring with a whisk until blended. Add ¼ cup granulated sugar and orange rind; stir well. Bring to a boil over medium heat; cook 1 minute or until thick, stirring constantly. Stir in juice; set aside.

4. Beat egg whites, cream of tartar, and salt with clean, dry beaters at high speed of a mixer until soft peaks form. Gradually add 2 tablespoons sugar, 1 tablespoon at a time, beating until stiff peaks form. Gently fold one-fourth egg white mixture into orange mixture; gently fold in remaining egg white mixture. Spoon into prepared soufflé dish.

5. Bake at 375° for 40 minutes or until puffy and set. Sprinkle with powdered sugar. Serve immediately. Yield: 4 servings.

POINTS: 3; **Exchanges:** 2 Starch
Per Serving: CAL 160 (6% from fat); PRO 6.4g; FAT 1.1g (sat 0.6g); CARB 31.5g; FIB 0.2g; CHOL 4mg; IRON 0.3mg; SOD 96mg; CALC 62mg

Apple-Glazed Dessert Pancake

1 tablespoon stick margarine
3 cups sliced Rome apple (about 1 pound)
1 tablespoon brown sugar
¾ teaspoon ground cinnamon
¼ teaspoon ground nutmeg
½ cup apple juice
¼ cup water
1 teaspoon cornstarch
1 cup all-purpose flour
2 cups 1% low-fat milk, divided
⅓ cup granulated sugar
2 teaspoons vanilla extract
¼ teaspoon salt
2 large eggs
2 large egg whites
Cooking spray
1 tablespoon powdered sugar

1. Preheat oven to 425°.

2. Melt margarine in a 10-inch cast-iron skillet over medium-high heat. Add apple; sauté 3 minutes. Stir in brown sugar, cinnamon, and nutmeg; cook 2 minutes. Combine juice, water, and cornstarch in a small bowl; stir well, and add to apple mixture. Bring to a boil; cook 1 minute or until thick, stirring gently. Remove apple mixture from skillet; set aside, and keep warm. Wipe skillet clean with a paper towel.

3. Place skillet in a 425° oven for 5 minutes. Combine flour and 1 cup milk; stir well with a whisk. Add remaining 1 cup milk, ⅓ cup granulated sugar, and next 4 ingredients; stir well. Remove skillet from oven; coat with cooking spray, and pour batter into skillet. Bake at 425° for 25 minutes or until puffy and brown around edges. Remove from oven; sprinkle with powdered sugar. Cut into wedges, and top with apple mixture. Serve immediately. Yield: 8 servings (serving size: 1 wedge pancake and ¼ cup apple topping).

POINTS: 4; **Exchanges**: 2 Starch, ½ Fruit
Per serving: CAL 196 (17% from fat); PRO 6.2g; FAT 3.8g (sat 1.2g); CARB 34.2g; FIB 1.8g; CHOL 58mg; IRON 1.2mg; SOD 151mg; CALC 93mg

Tiramisu

Try freezing Tiramisu for two hours before serving so it will cut cleanly.

⅔ cup sifted powdered sugar
1 (8-ounce) tub light cream cheese
1½ cups frozen reduced-calorie whipped topping, thawed and divided
½ cup granulated sugar
¼ cup water
3 large egg whites
½ cup hot water
1 tablespoon granulated sugar
1 tablespoon instant espresso coffee granules or 2 tablespoons instant coffee granules
2 tablespoons Kahlúa (coffee-flavored liqueur)
20 ladyfingers
½ teaspoon unsweetened cocoa

1. Combine sifted powdered sugar and light cream cheese in a bowl; beat at high speed of a mixer until well blended. Gently fold 1 cup whipped topping into cheese mixture.

2. Combine ½ cup granulated sugar, ¼ cup water, and egg whites in the top of a double boiler; place over simmering water. Beat at high speed of a mixer until stiff peaks form. Gently stir one-fourth

of egg white mixture into cheese mixture. Gently fold in remaining egg white mixture; set aside.

3. Combine hot water and next 3 ingredients; stir well. Split ladyfingers in half lengthwise. Arrange 20 ladyfinger halves, cut sides up, in bottom of an 8-inch square baking dish. Drizzle half of espresso mixture over ladyfinger halves. Spread half of cheese mixture over ladyfinger halves; repeat procedure with remaining ladyfinger halves, espresso mixture, and cheese mixture. Spread remaining ½ cup whipped topping evenly over cheese mixture; sprinkle with cocoa.

4. Place one toothpick in each corner and in center of Tiramisu to prevent plastic wrap from sticking to whipped topping; cover with plastic wrap. Chill 2 hours. Yield: 8 servings.

POINTS: 5; **Exchanges**: 1 Med-fat Meat, 2 Starch
Per serving: CAL 226 (28% from fat); PRO 4.7g; FAT 7g (sat 4.1g); CARB 30g; FIB 0g; CHOL 41mg; IRON 0.1mg; SOD 199mg; CALC 49

Nectarine-Pecan Pandowdy

6 cups peeled sliced nectarine
⅔ cup sugar
⅛ teaspoon ground cinnamon
Cooking spray
1 (4-ounce) can refrigerated crescent dinner rolls
1 tablespoon sugar
Sugared Pecans

1. Preheat oven to 350°.

2. Combine first 3 ingredients in a bowl; toss well. Spoon into a 9-inch pie plate coated with cooking spray. Bake at 350° for 15 minutes.

3. Unroll crescent roll dough, and separate along perforations into triangles; cut each triangle in half lengthwise. Remove nectarine mixture from oven, and arrange dough on top of hot mixture (dough will not cover entire surface). Lightly coat top of dough with cooking spray, and sprinkle with 1 tablespoon sugar. Bake at 350° for 20 minutes or until crust is lightly browned.

4. Remove from oven; gently press crust into nectarine mixture with a spoon, allowing juices to moisten top of crust. Sprinkle Sugared Pecans

Tiramisu, which means "pick-me-up" in Italian, refers to the coffee-liqueur mixture.

When you need a delicate dessert, serve Swedish Pancakes With Blackberry-Cassis Sauce.

cooking spray, spreading mixture evenly; let cool completely. Break into small pieces. Yield: ½ cup.

Swedish Pancakes With Blackberry-Cassis Sauce

2 large eggs, separated (at room temperature)
¼ teaspoon salt
1 tablespoon granulated sugar
1 tablespoon stick margarine, melted
½ teaspoon vanilla extract
½ cup all-purpose flour
⅛ teaspoon baking powder
1 cup skim milk
Cooking spray
Blackberry-Cassis Sauce
½ cup fresh blackberries
1½ teaspoons powdered sugar

1. Beat egg whites and salt with clean, dry beaters in a medium bowl at high speed of a mixer until stiff peaks form; set aside.
2. Combine egg yolks and granulated sugar in a large bowl; beat at high speed of a mixer until pale yellow (about 3 minutes). Add margarine and vanilla; beat well. Combine flour and baking powder. Add flour mixture to egg yolk mixture alternately with milk, beginning and ending with flour mixture. Add beaten egg whites, stirring gently with a whisk (batter will look separated).
3. Spoon 1 level tablespoon batter for each pancake onto a hot nonstick griddle or nonstick skillet coated with cooking spray. Turn pancakes when edges look cooked. Arrange 6 pancakes on each of 6 dessert plates. Drizzle ¼ cup Blackberry-Cassis Sauce over each serving; top with about 1 tablespoon fresh blackberries. Sift powdered sugar evenly over pancakes. Yield: 6 servings.

POINTS: 4; **Exchanges:** 2 Starch, 1 Fat
Per serving: CAL 204 (18% from fat); PRO 5g; FAT 4.1g (sat 1g); CARB 25.7g; FIB 2g; CHOL 67mg; IRON 0.8mg; SOD 170mg; CALC 80mg

Blackberry-Cassis Sauce:

1 cup fresh blackberries
3 tablespoons sugar
2 teaspoons cornstarch
⅛ teaspoon ground cinnamon

over crust, and bake 5 minutes. Serve warm. Yield: 6 servings (serving size: 1 cup).

POINTS: 6; **Exchanges:** 2½ Starch, 1 Fat, 1 Fruit
Per serving: CAL 290 (30% from fat); PRO 2.9g; FAT 9.8g (sat 1.5g); CARB 51.4g; FIB 3.4g; CHOL 0mg; IRON 0.5mg; SOD 166mg; CALC 12mg

Sugared Pecans:

1 tablespoon sugar
1 tablespoon stick margarine
¼ cup chopped pecans
1 tablespoon orange juice
¼ teaspoon ground cinnamon
Dash of ground red pepper
Cooking spray

1. Preheat oven to 350°.
2. Melt sugar and margarine in a small skillet over low heat. Remove from heat; stir in next 4 ingredients. Spread mixture evenly onto a baking sheet coated with cooking spray. Bake at 350° for 10 minutes, stirring after 5 minutes. Immediately scrape mixture onto a sheet of foil coated with

¾ cup orange juice
1 tablespoon fresh lemon juice
¼ cup crème de cassis (black currant-flavored liqueur)

1. Place blackberries in a food processor; process 1 minute or until puréed. Strain puréed berries through a sieve into a bowl, reserving blackberry juice; discard seeds. Add enough water to strained blackberry juice to yield ⅓ cup.

2. Combine sugar, cornstarch, and cinnamon in a saucepan. Add blackberry juice; stir with a whisk until blended. Stir in orange juice and lemon juice. Bring to a boil over medium heat; cook 1 minute, stirring constantly. Remove from heat; stir in crème de cassis. Serve warm. Yield: 1½ cups.

Creamy White Chocolate Dessert

¾ cup evaporated skim milk
½ cup sugar
3 (1-ounce) squares premium white baking chocolate, grated
2 teaspoons unflavored gelatin
¼ cup cold water
2 teaspoons vanilla extract
⅔ cup plain fat-free yogurt
¼ cup light sour cream
1 (8-ounce) container frozen reduced-calorie whipped topping, thawed
Cooking spray

1. Combine first 3 ingredients in a saucepan; stir with a whisk. Place over medium heat, and cook until white chocolate melts, stirring constantly. Pour into a medium bowl; let cool.

2. Sprinkle gelatin over ¼ cup cold water in a saucepan; let stand 1 minute. Place over low heat; cook until gelatin dissolves, stirring constantly. Pour gelatin mixture into white chocolate mixture; stir in vanilla. Cover; chill 30 minutes or until mixture reaches the consistency of unbeaten egg whites, stirring occasionally.

3. Combine yogurt and sour cream; add to white chocolate mixture, stirring gently with a whisk. Gently fold in whipped topping. Spoon mixture into an 11- x 7-inch baking dish coated with

cooking spray. Cover and chill at least 8 hours. Cut into squares. Yield: 12 servings.

POINTS: 3; **Exchanges:** 1½ Starch, 1 Fat
Per serving: CAL 147 (31% from fat); PRO 3.5g; FAT 5.1g (sat 1.3g); CARB 20.5g; FIB 0g; CHOL 3mg; IRON 0.1mg; SOD 53mg; CALC 107mg

Coffee Napoleons

2 teaspoons instant coffee granules
1 tablespoon hot water
1 (8-ounce) package Neufchâtel cheese or light cream cheese, softened
1¼ cups skim milk
1 (3.8-ounce) package fat-free chocolate-flavored instant pudding mix
1 cup frozen reduced-calorie whipped topping, thawed
36 wonton wrappers
butter-flavored cooking spray
½ cup granulated sugar
½ cup reduced-fat semisweet chocolate chips (about 3 ounces)
1½ tablespoons skim milk
1 teaspoon instant coffee granules
1 tablespoon powdered sugar

1. Preheat oven to 375°.

2. Dissolve 2 teaspoons coffee granules in 1 tablespoon hot water. Beat Neufchâtel cheese at medium speed of a mixer until creamy. Add coffee mixture, 1¼ cups milk, and pudding mix; beat at low speed until thick. Fold in whipped topping; cover and chill.

3. Coat both sides of each wonton wrapper with cooking spray; dredge in ½ cup granulated sugar. Arrange in a single layer on 2 jelly-roll pans lined with parchment paper. Bake at 375° for 3½ minutes; turn wrappers over, and bake an additional 1½ minutes or until edges are golden. Remove from pans; let cool on wire racks.

4. Combine chocolate chips, 1½ tablespoons milk, and 1 teaspoon coffee granules in a saucepan. Place over low heat; cook until chips melt, stirring constantly. Let cool slightly; spoon into a small zip-top plastic bag, and seal bag. Snip a tiny hole in one corner of bag using scissors. Pipe chocolate mixture evenly over 12 wonton wrappers. Spoon

1. Preheat oven to 400°.

2. Combine flour and next 5 ingredients in a bowl; cut in margarine with a pastry blender or 2 knives until mixture resembles coarse meal. Add buttermilk and egg, stirring just until moist (dough will be sticky).

3. Turn dough out onto a lightly floured surface; with floured hands, knead lightly 4 times. Pat dough into a 10-inch circle on a baking sheet coated with cooking spray. Cut dough into 10 wedges, cutting into, but not through, dough. Bake at 400° for 15 minutes or until golden.

4. Combine hot water and instant coffee granules in a small bowl; stir well. Add powdered sugar; stir well. Drizzle over warm scones. Cut into 10 wedges; top each with 1 walnut half. Serve warm. Yield: 10 servings.

POINTS: 5; **Exchanges:** 2½ Starch, 1 Fat
Per serving: CAL 220 (30% from fat); PRO 4g; FAT 7.4g (sat 1.4g); CARB 34.7g; FIB 0.7g; CHOL 24mg; IRON 1.4mg; SOD 194mg; CALC 73mg

Brandied Prune Turnovers

2   cups chopped pitted prunes (about ¾ pound)
½   cup water
6   tablespoons brandy
1   tablespoon water
1   teaspoon cornstarch
6   tablespoons brown sugar
6   tablespoons chopped almonds or pecans, toasted
12   sheets frozen phyllo dough, thawed
Butter-flavored cooking spray
1   tablespoon powdered sugar

1. Preheat oven to 350°.

2. Combine chopped prunes, ½ cup water, and brandy in a small saucepan; bring to a boil. Reduce heat; simmer, uncovered, 5 minutes. Combine 1 tablespoon water and cornstarch; stir well. Add cornstarch mixture to prune mixture; stir well. Stir in brown sugar. Bring to a boil, and cook 1 minute, stirring constantly. Remove from heat, and let cool. Stir in nuts.

3. Working with 1 phyllo sheet at a time, heavily

Turn your kitchen into a trendy coffeehouse by serving Gingersnap Scones With Espresso Glaze and a cup of joe.

half of cheese mixture evenly on 12 plain wonton wrappers; top each with another plain wonton wrapper. Spoon remaining half of filling evenly on top of plain wrappers; top with chocolate-drizzled wrappers. Sift powdered sugar evenly over pastries. Serve immediately. Yield: 12 servings.

POINTS: 5; **Exchanges:** 2½ Starch, ½ Fat
Per serving: CAL 217 (26% from fat); PRO 5.4g; FAT 6.3g (sat 3.1g); CARB 34.7g; FIB 0g; CHOL 17mg; IRON 3.4mg; SOD 348mg; CALC 103mg

Gingersnap Scones With Espresso Glaze

1¾ cups all-purpose flour
¼   cup gingersnap crumbs (about 6 cookies)
¼   cup granulated sugar
1½ teaspoons baking powder
½   teaspoon baking soda
¼   teaspoon salt
¼   cup chilled stick margarine, cut into small pieces
½   cup low-fat buttermilk
1   large egg, lightly beaten
Cooking spray
1   tablespoon hot water
1½ teaspoons instant coffee granules
¾   cup sifted powdered sugar
10   walnut halves

coat each sheet with cooking spray. Stack 1 phyllo sheet on top of another; coat top sheet with cooking spray. Using a pizza cutter or scissors, cut stack lengthwise into 4 (3½-inch-wide) strips.

4. Spoon about 1½ tablespoons prune mixture on 1 short side of each phyllo strip, and fold left bottom corner over mixture forming a triangle. Keep folding back and forth into triangle to end of strip. Repeat procedure with remaining sheets of phyllo and prune mixture.

5. Place triangles, seam sides down, on a baking sheet coated with cooking spray. Lightly spray turnovers with cooking spray. Bake at 350° for 20 minutes or until golden. Let cool completely on a wire rack. Sift powdered sugar over turnovers. Yield: 2 dozen (serving size: 2 turnovers).

POINTS: 4; **Exchanges:** 1 Starch, ½ Fat
Per serving: CAL 196 (19% from fat); PRO 2.8g; FAT 4.2g (sat 0.5g); CARB 33.2g; FIB 0.8g; CHOL 0mg; IRON 1.5mg; SOD 107mg; CALC 28mg

Cesnica

Butter-flavored cooking spray
6   sheets frozen phyllo dough, thawed
¾   cup golden raisins
6   tablespoons chopped walnuts, toasted
2   tablespoons stick margarine, melted
½   cup honey
¼   cup water
1   teaspoon fresh lemon juice

1. Preheat oven to 350°.

2. Coat an 8-inch round cake pan with cooking spray; set aside.

3. Stack phyllo sheets; cut in half crosswise. Gently press 1 half-sheet of phyllo into cake pan, allowing ends to extend over edges of pan; lightly coat phyllo with cooking spray. Place another half-sheet of phyllo across first sheet to form a crisscross design; lightly coat phyllo with cooking spray. Repeat procedure with another half-sheet of phyllo and cooking spray.

4. Sprinkle 2 tablespoons raisins and 1 tablespoon walnuts over phyllo. Place another half-sheet of phyllo in pan, continuing crisscross design; lightly coat phyllo with cooking spray. Sprinkle 2 tablespoons raisins and 1 tablespoon walnut over phyllo. Repeat procedure with 5 half-sheets of phyllo, cooking spray, remaining raisins, and remaining walnuts, ending with phyllo coated with cooking spray.

5. Lightly coat 1 side of remaining 3 half-sheets of phyllo; gently layer each into cake pan to form a crisscross design, allowing ends to extend over edges of pan. Fold in edges of phyllo to fit pan and form a rim.

6. Score diamond shapes into top layers of phyllo, using a sharp knife. Drizzle margarine over phyllo. Bake at 350° for 25 minutes.

7. Combine honey, water, and lemon juice in a saucepan; bring to a boil. Reduce heat; simmer, uncovered, 10 minutes, stirring frequently. Remove from heat; drizzle honey mixture over phyllo. Let cool completely in pan. Cut into wedges. Yield: 10 servings.

POINTS: 4; **Exchanges:** 2 Starch, ½ Fat
Per serving: CAL 179 (29% from fat); PRO 2.9g; FAT 5.4g (sat 0.7g); CARB 32.4g; FIB 0.8g; CHOL 0mg; IRON 0.7mg; SOD 29mg; CALC 11mg

Traditionally, a foil-wrapped coin is tucked somewhere inside Cesnica, a Yugoslavian version of Baklava.

OH, SWEET PRUNE

Prune butter works well in baked products because it not only sweetens but also replaces fat. We used the Lekvar brand, which may be found with jams and jellies in supermarkets and is also available from Sokol and Company, 5315 Dansher Road, Countryside, IL 60525; (708) 482-8250.

You can substitute baby food or the following homemade prune butter: Combine ⅓ cup pitted prunes, 1 teaspoon sugar, and 2 teaspoons light-colored corn syrup in a food processor; process 5 seconds. With processor on, slowly add 2 tablespoons water through food chute; process until mixture is smooth, scraping sides of bowl frequently.

Maple-Cranberry Baked Apples

Use real maple syrup instead of pancake syrup. The flavor is worth the extra cost.

2½ cups cranberry juice cocktail
½   cup maple syrup
¼   cup firmly packed light brown sugar
1   tablespoon lemon juice
2   teaspoons peeled grated fresh ginger
1   teaspoon ground cinnamon
1   teaspoon cornstarch
1   teaspoon vanilla extract
8   medium Rome apples, cored
¾   cup dried cranberries or raisins
¼   cup chopped pecans
¼   cup shaved white chocolate

1. Preheat oven to 350°.

2. Combine first 8 ingredients in a large bowl; stir well, and set aside.

3. Peel top half of each apple, and place in a shallow roasting pan. Fill centers of apples evenly with dried cranberries and pecans. Pour cranberry juice mixture over apples. Bake at 350° for 1 hour or until tender, basting apples twice with syrup from pan. Place apples on dessert plates, and drizzle evenly with remaining syrup. Sprinkle with white chocolate. Yield: 8 servings (serving size: 1 apple, 2 tablespoons syrup, and 1½ teaspoons white chocolate).

POINTS: 5; **Exchanges:** 2 Fruit, 2 Starch
Per serving: CAL 286 (14% from fat); PRO 1.2g; FAT 4.6g (sat 1.2g); CARB 64g; FIB 4.4g; CHOL 0mg; IRON 1mg; SOD 13mg; CALC 47mg

Praline Bananas Foster

If you don't care for praline liqueur or don't have it on hand, you can always substitute ¼ to ½ teaspoon rum extract.

¼   cup firmly packed dark brown sugar
1½ teaspoons cornstarch
½   cup evaporated skim milk
2   tablespoons chopped pecans, toasted
1   tablespoon praline liqueur or dark rum
2   teaspoons reduced-calorie stick margarine
1   teaspoon vanilla extract
2   medium firm ripe bananas
2   cups vanilla low-fat frozen yogurt

1. Combine brown sugar and cornstarch in a medium saucepan. Gradually add milk, stirring until blended. Bring to a boil over medium heat, and cook until mixture thickens slightly. Remove from heat. Add pecans, liqueur, margarine, and vanilla, stirring until margarine melts. Remove from heat; set aside.

2. Cut each banana in half crosswise; cut each piece in half lengthwise. Spoon ½ cup frozen yogurt into each of 4 dessert dishes. Top each serving with 2 banana pieces, and drizzle with 3 tablespoons praline sauce. Yield: 4 servings.

POINTS: 6; **Exchanges:** 1½ Starch, 1 Fat, ½ Sk Milk
Per serving: CAL 272 (20% from fat); PRO 6.2g; FAT 6g (sat 1.4g); CARB 49.8g; FIB 2g; CHOL 11mg; IRON 0.6mg; SOD 95mg; CALC 205mg

Black-Bottom Cheesecake Cups

To toast chopped almonds, spread in a single layer in a shallow baking dish and bake at 300° for 15 minutes, stirring occasionally.

1½ cups all-purpose flour
¾   cup granulated sugar
⅓   cup unsweetened cocoa
1   tablespoon instant coffee granules
1   teaspoon baking soda
½   teaspoon salt
⅓   cup prune butter or 1 (4-ounce) jar prune baby food
1   cup water
1   tablespoon white vinegar
2   teaspoons vanilla extract
1   (8-ounce) block fat-free cream cheese, softened
½   cup sifted powdered sugar
1   large egg
Cooking spray
½   cup semisweet chocolate chips
¼   cup chopped almonds, toasted

1. Preheat oven to 350°.

2. Combine first 6 ingredients in a large bowl. Combine prune butter, water, vinegar, and vanilla; stir well. Add to flour mixture, stirring with a whisk until blended; set chocolate batter aside.

3. Beat cream cheese in a bowl at medium speed of a mixer until smooth. Add powdered sugar and egg, beating until well blended; set cream cheese mixture aside.

4. Place 18 paper muffin cup liners in muffin

Black-Bottom
Cheesecake Cups

cups; coat liners with cooking spray. Divide chocolate batter evenly among muffin cups; spoon cream cheese mixture evenly on top of chocolate batter in each cup. Sprinkle chocolate chips and almonds over cream cheese mixture. Bake at 350° for 25 minutes or until a wooden pick inserted in center comes out clean. Let cool in pans 5 minutes on a wire rack; remove from pans, and let cool completely on wire rack. Yield: 1½ dozen (serving size: 1 cheesecake cup).

POINTS: 3; **Exchanges:** 1½ Starch, ½ Fat
Per serving: CAL 151 (21% from fat); PRO 4.2g; FAT 3.5g (sat 1.3g); CARB 26.1g; FIB 0.7g; CHOL 14mg; IRON 1mg; SOD 192mg; CALC 50mg

Honey-Baked Figs

12 dried figs
⅓ cup honey
2 tablespoons slivered almonds, toasted

1. Preheat oven to 325°.
2. Place figs in a saucepan. Add water to cover; bring to a boil. Cover, reduce heat, and simmer 20 minutes. Remove from heat; uncover and let stand 20 minutes. Drain well. Place figs in a 1½-quart baking dish; drizzle with honey. Bake at 325° for 25 minutes or until thoroughly heated, stirring occasionally. Sprinkle with toasted almonds. Serve warm. Yield: 4 servings (serving size: 3 figs).

POINTS: 3; **Exchanges:** 3 Fruit, 1 Starch
Per serving: CAL 253 (10% from fat); PRO 2.6g; FAT 2.8g (sat 0.3g); CARB 60.8g; FIB 10g; CHOL 0mg; IRON 1.5mg; SOD 8mg; CALC 93mg

Cocoa-Peanut Butter Banana Bites

4 small firm ripe bananas (about 1 pound)
½ cup crispy wheat cereal squares (such as Wheat Chex), crushed
1 tablespoon creamy peanut butter
1 tablespoon honey
1 teaspoon unsweetened cocoa

1. Cut bananas in half lengthwise; set aside.
2. Combine crushed cereal and next 3 ingredients; stir well. Spread 1 tablespoon cereal mixture

over cut sides of 4 banana halves; top with remaining banana halves. Cut each crosswise into 6 pieces. Serve immediately. Yield: 8 servings (serving size: 3 pieces).

POINTS: 1; **Exchanges:** ½ Fruit, ½ Starch
Per serving: CAL 84 (15% from fat); PRO 1.5g; FAT 1.4g (sat 0.3g); CARB 18.3g; FIB 2g; CHOL 0mg; IRON 0.7mg; SOD 30mg; CALC 6mg

Caramel Pears

⅓ cup orange juice
3 tablespoons brown sugar
⅛ teaspoon ground cinnamon
Dash of ground cloves
2 Bosc pears, each peeled, cored, and cut into 1-inch-thick wedges
2 tablespoons white rum
Cinnamon sticks (optional)

1. Combine first 4 ingredients in a medium saucepan, and bring to a boil. Reduce heat; simmer, uncovered, 5 minutes. Add pears, and cook 10 minutes or until tender. Add rum; cook 1 minute. Divide pears and sauce evenly between 2 dessert dishes. Garnish with cinnamon sticks, if desired. Yield: 2 servings.

POINTS: 1; **Exchanges:** 1½ Fruit, 1 Starch
Per serving: CAL 162 (4% from fat); PRO 0.9g; FAT 0.7g (sat 0g); CARB 41.4g; FIB 4.2g; CHOL 0mg; IRON 0.7mg; SOD 6mg; CALC 34mg

Strawberries Romanoff

If you don't have Cointreau, use an equal amount of frozen orange juice concentrate.

3 cups fresh strawberries, hulled
2 tablespoons powdered sugar
1 tablespoon Cointreau (orange-flavored liqueur)
1 cup vanilla fat-free frozen yogurt, softened
¼ cup fat-free sour cream

1. Combine fresh strawberries, powdered sugar, and orange-flavored liqueur in a medium bowl; toss gently. Cover and chill at least 1 hour.
2. Combine fat-free frozen yogurt and fat-free sour cream in a small bowl, stirring until mixture is smooth. Spoon strawberries evenly into 4 individual dessert dishes. Spoon yogurt mix-

ture evenly over strawberries. Serve immediately. Yield: 4 servings.

POINTS: 2; **Exchanges:** 1 Fruit, ½ Starch
Per serving: CAL 116 (3% from fat); PRO 3.6g; FAT 0.4g (sat 0g); CARB 23.7g; FIB 2.9g; CHOL 0mg; IRON 0.4mg; SOD 45mg; CALC 87mg

Cheesy Apple Pie in a Glass

4   cups peeled thinly sliced Red Delicious apple (about 2 apples)
⅔   cup apple juice
¼   cup firmly packed brown sugar
3   tablespoons raisins
1   teaspoon ground cinnamon
½   teaspoon ground nutmeg
½   teaspoon ground allspice, divided
1½   teaspoons vanilla extract
¼   teaspoon rum extract
3   ounces mascarpone cheese
¾   cup low-fat cinnamon crisp graham cracker crumbs (about 8 crackers), divided
1   cup vanilla fat-free frozen yogurt
Mascarpone cheese (optional)

1. Combine first 6 ingredients and ¼ teaspoon allspice in a medium saucepan. Cook over medium-low heat 20 minutes or until apples are tender and mixture is slightly thick. Remove from heat; let cool. Stir in remaining ¼ teaspoon allspice, extracts, and 3 ounces mascarpone cheese.
2. Spoon ¼ cup apple mixture into each of 4 parfait glasses, and sprinkle each with 1½ tablespoons crumbs. Top each with ¼ cup yogurt, ¼ cup apple mixture, and 1½ tablespoons crumbs. Garnish with additional mascarpone cheese, if desired. Serve immediately. Yield: 4 servings.

POINTS: 7; **Exchanges:** 3 Starch, 1½ Fat, 1 Fruit
Per serving: CAL 339 (29% from fat); PRO 4.3g; FAT 11.1g (sat 5.5g); CARB 57.8g; FIB 3.8g; CHOL 19mg; IRON 1.2mg; SOD 124mg; CALC 144mg

Orange-Filled Ladyfingers

1¼   cups frozen reduced-calorie whipped topping, thawed
2   drops yellow food coloring
2   drops red food coloring
24   ladyfingers
¼   cup Grand Marnier (orange-flavored liqueur)
½   cup fat-free hot fudge topping

Orange rind strips (optional)
Fresh mint sprigs (optional)

1. Combine first 3 ingredients in a bowl; stir gently with a whisk until blended. Set aside.
2. Split ladyfingers in half lengthwise. Brush cut sides of ladyfingers with Grand Marnier.
3. Spread whipped topping mixture evenly over bottom halves of ladyfingers. Cover with top halves of ladyfingers. Spoon fudge sauce into a small zip-top plastic bag; seal bag. Snip a tiny hole in one corner of bag using scissors. Pipe about 2 teaspoons fudge sauce on top of each filled ladyfinger. Garnish with orange rind strips and mint sprigs, if desired. Yield: 2 dozen (serving size: 1 filled ladyfinger).

POINTS: 1; **Exchanges:** ½ Starch
Per serving: CAL 53 (15% from fat); PRO 1g; FAT 0.9g (sat 0.5g); CARB 9.4g; FIB 0.3g; CHOL 13mg; IRON 0.4mg; SOD 72mg; CALC 7mg

For a little bit of whimsy, try Cheesy Apple Pie in a Glass, a zingy-tasting dessert spiced with imagination.

allspice A pea-size berry from the pimiento tree, named because it tastes like a combination of cloves, cinnamon, and nutmeg. It can be purchased as whole berries or ground, and is used in both savory and sweet dishes.

Arborio rice An Italian-grown grain containing a high starch content. Traditionally it is used for risotto.

amaretto An almond-flavored liqueur originally from Italy.

Bundt pan A tube pan with fluted sides.

buttercup squash A type of turban squash with a light blue-gray to dark green shell and orange flesh. It has a flavor similar to the sweet potato.

cake flour A soft-wheat flour with a fine texture and high starch content. Also called pastry flour, it is used to produce very tender cakes and pastries.

crème de cassis A black currant-flavored liqueur.

currants Dried seedless Zante grapes resembling tiny raisins.

Dutch process cocoa A rich, dark cocoa treated with an alkali, such as baking soda, making it less acidic than regular cocoa.

ginger A common spice known for its peppery and sweet flavor. Ginger comes in several forms: fresh (the gnarled root), dried ground, crystallized, bottled chopped, and pickled.

Grand Marnier A brandy-based, orange-flavored French liqueur. It is translucent and dark golden in appearance.

Kahlúa A Mexican coffee-flavored liqueur.

kiwifruit A small oblong fruit that has a rough brown covering on the outside and bright-green flesh flecked with tiny edible black seeds inside. Eaten peeled, the fruit tastes similar to pineapple and strawberry.

mango A juicy, exotically sweet fruit with fragrant, golden flesh. The flesh must be carefully carved away from the huge flat seed that traverses the length of the fruit.

molasses The brownish-black syrup produced during the refining of sugar cane and sugar beets.

Neufchâtel cheese A soft, white, unripened cheese similar to cream cheese.

phyllo dough A tissue-thin pastry dough generally used in layers and typically used in the preparation of baklava.

polenta A northern Italian staple made from cooking cornmeal with milk or water until thick.

ramekin A baking dish, usually made of porcelain or earthenware, that resembles a miniature soufflé dish.

rhubarb A thick, celerylike vegetable ranging in color from pink to cherry red. It is often cooked with a sweetener to cut the natural tartness of the plant. Rhubarb is commonly used as a fruit in desserts.

semolina flour A coarsely ground durum wheat flour used in the making of pasta.

turbinado sugar A coarse sugar that is blond in color and has a slight molasses flavor.

zest The aromatic, colored portion of the skin of citrus fruit (but not the white pith).

Nutrition and Serving-Size Information

Here are some specific guidelines that *Weight Watchers* Magazine adheres to regarding our recipes. For nutritional accuracy, please be sure to follow our suggestions.

• When preparing a recipe that yields more than one serving, it is important to mix the ingredients well and then divide the mixture evenly.

• Where liquid and solid parts have to be divided evenly, drain the liquid and set it aside. Evenly divide the remaining ingredients; then add equal amounts of the liquid to each serving.

• Unless otherwise indicated, servings of meat, poultry, and fish refer to cooked, skinned, and boned servings.

• Recipes provide approximate nutritional information, including the following: CAL (calories), PRO (protein), FAT (total fat), sat (saturated fat), CARB (carbohydrates), FIB (dietary fiber), CHOL (cholesterol), IRON (iron), SOD (sodium), and CALC (calcium). Measurements are abbreviated as follows: g (grams), mg (milligrams).

• Recipes include *POINTS*® based on Weight Watchers International's 1•2•3 Success® Weight Loss Plan.

• *POINTS* are calculated from a formula based on calories, fat, and fiber that assigns higher points to higher-calorie, higher-fat foods. Based on your present weight, you are allowed a certain amount of *POINTS* per day.

Note: Because data on fat distribution are not available for some processed foods, these breakdowns should be considered approximate.

• Recipes now include diabetic exchanges, which have been calculated from the *Exchange List for Meal Planning* developed by The American Dietetic Association and the American Diabetes Association. The exchange information is designated as follows: starch, fruit, skim milk (sk milk), low-fat milk (l-f milk), whole milk (wh milk), vegetable (veg), very lean meat, lean meat, medium-fat meat (med-fat meat), high-fat meat (hi-fat meat), and fat.

Each category from the exchange list consists of foods that are similar in their nutritional makeup. Therefore, foods within the same category can be substituted. For example, ½ cup cereal for one slice of bread.

• The recipes that are shown in our photographs may vary as to the number of servings pictured. It is important that you refer to the recipes for the exact serving information.

USEFUL EQUIVALENTS FOR TEMPERATURE SETTINGS

	Fahrenheit	Celsius	Gas Mark
Freeze Water	32° F	0°C	
Room Temperature	68° F	20° C	
Boil Water	212° F	100° C	
Bake	325° F	160° C	3
	350° F	180° C	4
	375° F	190° C	5
	400° F	200° C	6
	425° F	220° C	7
	450° F	230° C	8
Broil			Grill

Cakes

Blueberry-Buttermilk Cake 20
Brownie Snack Cake 10
Caramel-Pineapple Upside-Down Cake 9
Chocolate Pound Cake 10
Chocolate Roulade With Raspberries 15
Cinnamon-Apple Cake 12
Dark-Chocolate Soufflé Cake 11
Fruited Carrot Cake 20
Honey Cake 20
Irish Fruitcake 16
Lemon Chiffon Cake With Fresh-Fruit
  Compote 11
Mississippi Mud Cake 17
New York Cheesecake 15
Oat Cake With Coconut-Nut Topping 13
Orange-Coconut Angel Food Cake 9
Polenta Cake With Roasted Nectarines 18
Raspberry Almond Coffeecake 21
Rich Chocolate Layer Cake 19
Semolina Pudding Cake 12
Spiced Pumpkin Cake 17
Triple-Chocolate Cheesecake 14

Cookies

Almond Chess Squares 43
Apple-Spice Bars 46
Banana-Macadamia Madeleines 41
Basic Icebox Sugar Cookies 52
Benne Seed Wafers 45
Cappuccino Crinkles 42
Chocolate-Nut Popcorn Clusters 51
Chocolate-Pine Nut Meringue Smooches 52
Double-Chocolate Chews 48
Easy Peanut Butter Cookies 46
Frosted Peppermint Brownies 49
Fudgy Cream Cheese Brownies 46
Giant Gingersnaps 51
Hamantaschen 50
Lemon Squares 45
Molasses-Spice Crackles 45
No-Bake Fig Bars 50
Oatmeal-Raisin Cookies 41
Peanut Butter-Oat Squares 51
Snappy Almond Stars 48
Soft Spice Biscotti 42
Sweet Cornmeal Cookies 43
Thumbprint Cookies 42
Vanilla Wafers 48
White Chocolate Chip Cookies 41

Custards and Puddings

Banana Pudding 56
Butterscotch Tapioca 57
Caramelized Sweet Potato Pudding 58
Cherry Clafouti 64
Citrus Sponge Pudding 63
Cream Cheese Brûlée With
  Raspberries 63
Creamy Buttercup Pudding 64
Crème Caramel 59
Double-Chocolate Satin Pudding 64
Fig Bar Bread Pudding With Amaretto
  Sauce 61
Lemon-Rosemary Custard Cakes 59
Maple Rice Pudding 58
New England Corn Pudding With Maple
  Syrup Sauce 57
Queen of Puddings 65
Steamed Chocolate Pudding With
  Brandied Cherry Sauce 56
Summer Fruit With Custard Sauce 61
Sweet Kugel 63
Sweet Potato Flan 62
Vanilla Pudding 62

Frozen Desserts

Apricot-Yogurt Tortoni 70
Baked Alaska 69
Bourbon-Raisin Ice Cream 72
Café au Lait Granita 78
Caramel Ice Cream Dessert 77
Coffee-Toffee Dessert 75
Daiquiri Ice With Kiwifruit 72
Frozen Chocolate Roulage 73
Frozen Chocolate-Cherry Squares 75
Frozen Mud Pie Sandwiches 76
Frozen Raspberry Brownie Bars 73
Frozen Strawberry Dessert 71
Frozen Strawberry Margarita Squares 77
Frozen Yogurt With Rum-Raisin
  Sauce 78
Ginger-Mango Gelato 70
Kona Coffee Ice Cream in Chocolate
  Cookie Cups 70
Lemon Ice 69
Maple-Rum Banana Sundaes 75
Praline-Chocolate Bombe 76
Strawberry-Champagne Sorbet 72
Vanilla-Buttermilk Ice Cream 77

Pies and Cobblers

Apple Slump With Nutmeg Sauce 29
Apple-Cranberry Crumble 29
Banana Cream Pie 30
Blackberry Cobbler 30
Blueberry Grunt 33
Brownie Cheese Pie 26
Butterscotch Cream Pie 36
Cherry Cobbler 37
Cherry Ping 27
Chocolate Meringue Pie 28
Chocolate-Mint Ice Cream Pie 35
Cranberry-Chocolate Crumble 29
Double-Chocolate Cream Tart 33
Dried-Fruit Cobbler With Molasses
  Biscuits 34
Gingered Apricot Crumble 26
Honey-Rhubarb Crumble 32
Maple-Pecan Tart 32
Peach-and-Blueberry Cobbler 27
Pumpkin-Praline Pie 36
Raspberry Chiffon Pie 25
Streusel Apple Pie 24
Sweet Potato-Bourbon Tart 35
Tropical Sundae Pie 25

Still More Sweets

Apple-Glazed Dessert Pancake 83
Black-Bottom Cheesecake Cups 90
Brandied Prune Turnovers 88
Cantaloupe and Blackberries With
  Almond Cream 82
Caramel Pears 92
Cesnica 89
Cheesy Apple Pie in a Glass 93
Cocoa-Peanut Butter Banana Bites 92
Creamy White Chocolate Dessert 87
Gingered Pear and Plum Brown Betty 87
Gingersnap Scones With Espresso Glaze 88
Honey-Baked Figs 92
Maple-Cranberry Baked Apples 90
Nectarine-Pecan Pandowdy 84
Orange-Filled Ladyfingers 93
Orange Soufflé 83
Pavlova 82
Praline Bananas Foster 90
Razzle-Dazzle Berry Trifle 83
Strawberries Romanoff 92
Swedish Pancakes With Blackberry-Cassis
  Sauce 86
Tiramisu 84